Online Ecological
and Environmental Data

Online Ecological and Environmental Data has been co-published simultaneously as *Science & Technology Libraries,* Volume 23, Number 4 2003.

Science & Technology Libraries Monographic "Separates"

Below is a list of "separates," which in serials librarianship means a special issue simultaneously published as a special journal issue or double-issue *and* as a "separate" hardbound monograph. (This is a format which we also call a "DocuSerial.")

"Separates" are published because specialized libraries or professionals may wish to purchase a specific thematic issue by itself in a format which can be separately cataloged and shelved, as opposed to purchasing the journal on an on-going basis. Faculty members may also more easily consider a "separate" for classroom adoption.

"Separates" are carefully classified separately with the major book jobbers so that the journal tie-in can be noted on new book order slips to avoid duplicate purchasing.

You may wish to visit Haworth's website at . . .

http://www.HaworthPress.com

. . . to search our online catalog for complete tables of contents of these separates and related publications.

You may also call 1-800-HAWORTH (outside US/Canada: 607-722-5857), or Fax: 1-800-895-0582 (outside US/Canada: 607-771-0012), or e-mail at:

docdelivery@haworthpress.com

Online Ecological and Environmental Data, edited by Virginia Baldwin, MS, MLS (Vol. 23, No. 4, 2003). *Explores aspects of the online data projects developed in various fields from ecological and environmental research programs.*

Leadership and Management Principles in Libraries in Developing Countries, edited by Wei Wei, MS, MLS, Sue O'Neill, BA, MLS, MPA, and Sylvia E. A. Piggott, BA, MLS (Vol. 23, No. 2/3, 2002). *Examines case studies of innovative programs from special libraries in developing countries, with a focus on the management and leadership skills that made these initiatives successful.*

Scholarly Communication in Science and Engineering Research in Higher Education, edited by Wei Wei, MA, MLS (Vol. 22, No. 3/4, 2002). *Examines science and technology libraries' difficulties with maintaining expensive journal subscriptions for both researchers and tenure-ready scholars; offers advice and examples of efficient improvements to make fact-finding and publication easier and more cost-efficient.*

Patents and Trademark Information: Uses and Perspectives, edited by Virginia Baldwin, MS, MLS (Vol. 22, No. 1/2, 2001). *"A lucid and in-depth presentation of key resources and information systems in this area." (Javed Mostafa, PhD, Victor H. Yngve Associate Professor, Indiana University, Bloomington)*

Information and the Professional Scientist and Engineer, edited by Virginia Baldwin, MS, MLS, and Julie Hallmark, PhD (Vol. 21, No. 3/4, 2001). *Covers information needs, information seeking, communication behavior, and information resources.*

Information Practice in Science and Technology: Evolving Challenges and New Directions, edited by Mary C. Schlembach, BS, MLS, CAS (Vol. 21, No. 1/2, 2001). *Shows how libraries are addressing new challenges and changes in today's publishing market, in interdisciplinary research areas, and in online access.*

Electronic Resources and Services in Sci-Tech Libraries, edited by Mary C. Schlembach, BS, MLS, and William H. Mischo, BA, MA (Vol. 20, No. 2/3, 2001). *Examines collection development, reference service, and information service in science and technology libraries.*

Engineering Libraries: Building Collections and Delivering Services, edited by Thomas W. Conkling, BS, MLS, and Linda R. Musser, BS, MS (Vol. 19, No. 3/4, 2001). *"Highly useful. The range of topics is broad, from collections to user services . . . most of the authors provide extra value by focusing on points of special interest. Of value to almost all librarians or information specialists in academic or special libraries, or as a supplementary text for graduate library courses." (Susan Davis Herring, MLS, PhD, Engineering Reference Librarian, M. Louis Salmon Library, University of Alabama, Huntsville)*

Electronic Expectations: Science Journals on the Web, by Tony Stankus, MLS (Vol. 18, No. 2/3, 1999). *Separates the hype about electronic journals from the realities that they will bring. This book provides a complete tutorial review of the literature that relates to the rise of electronic journals in the sciences and explores the many cost factors that may prevent electronic journals from becoming revolutionary in the research industry.*

Digital Libraries: Philosophies, Technical Design Considerations, and Example Scenarios, edited by David Stern (Vol. 17, No. 3/4, 1999). "Digital Libraries: Philosophies, Technical Design Considerations, and Example Scenarios *targets the general librarian population and does a good job of opening eyes to the impact that digital library projects are already having in our automated libraries." (Kimberly J. Parker, MILS, Electronic Publishing & Collections Librarian, Yale University Library)*

Sci/Tech Librarianship: Education and Training, edited by Julie Hallmark, PhD, and Ruth K. Seidman, MSLS (Vol. 17, No. 2, 1998). *"Insightful, informative, and right-on-the-mark. . . . This collection provides a much-needed view of the education of sci/tech librarians." (Michael R. Leach, AB, Director, Physics Research Library, Harvard University)*

Chemical Librarianship: Challenges and Opportunities, edited by Arleen N. Somerville (Vol. 16, No. 3/4, 1997). *"Presents a most satisfying collection of articles that will be of interest, first and foremost, to chemistry librarians, but also to science librarians working in other science disciplines within academic settings." (Barbara List, Director, Science and Engineering Libraries, Columbia University, New York, New York)*

History of Science and Technology: A Sampler of Centers and Collections of Distinction, edited by Cynthia Steinke, MS (Vol. 14, No. 4, 1995). *"A 'grand tour' of history of science and technology collections that is of great interest to scholars, students and librarians." (Jay K. Lucker, AB, MSLS, Director of Libraries, Massachusetts Institute of Technology; Lecturer in Science and Technology, Simmons College, Graduate School of Library and Information Science)*

Instruction for Information Access in Sci-Tech Libraries, edited by Cynthia Steinke, MS (Vol. 14, No. 2, 1994). *"A refreshing mix of user education programs and contain[s] many examples of good practice." (Library Review and Reference Reviews)*

Scientific and Clinical Literature for the Decade of the Brain, edited by Tony Stankus, MLS (Vol. 13, No. 3/4, 1993). *"This format combined with selected book and journal title lists is very convenient for life science, social science, or general reference librarians/bibliographers who wish to review the area or get up to speed quickly." (Ruth Lewis, MLS, Biology Librarian, Washington University, St. Louis, Missouri)*

Sci-Tech Libraries of the Future, edited by Cynthia Steinke, MS (Vol. 12, No. 4 and Vol. 13, No. 1, 1993). *"Very timely. . . . Will be of interest to all libraries confronted with changes in technology, information formats, and user expectations." (LA Record)*

Science Librarianship at America's Liberal Arts Colleges: Working Librarians Tell Their Stories, edited by Tony Stankus, MLS (Vol. 12, No. 3, 1992). *"For those teetering on the tightrope between the needs and desires of science faculty and liberal arts librarianship, this book brings a sense of balance." (Teresa R. Faust, MLS, Science Reference Librarian, Wake Forest University)*

Biographies of Scientists for Sci-Tech Libraries: Adding Faces to the Facts, edited by Tony Stankus, MLS (Vol. 11, No. 4, 1992). *"A guide to biographies of scientists from a wide variety of scientific fields, identifying titles that reveal the personality of the biographee as well as contributions to his/her field." (Sci Tech Book News)*

Information Seeking and Communicating Behavior of Scientists and Engineers, edited by Cynthia Steinke, MS (Vol. 11, No. 3, 1991). *"Unequivocally recommended. . . . The subject is one of importance to most university libraries, which are actively engaged in addressing user needs as a framework for library services." (New Library World)*

Technology Transfer: The Role of the Sci-Tech Librarian, edited by Cynthia Steinke, MS (Vol. 11, No. 2, 1991). *"Educates the reader about the role of information professionals in the multifaceted technology transfer process." (Journal of Chemical Information and Computer Sciences)*

Electronic Information Systems in Sci-Tech Libraries, edited by Cynthia Steinke, MS (Vol. 11, No. 1, 1990). *"Serves to illustrate the possibilities for effective networking from any library/information facility to any other geographical point." (Library Journal)*

The Role of Trade Literature in Sci-Tech Libraries, edited by Ellis Mount, DLS (Vol. 10, No. 4, 1990). *"A highly useful resource to identify and discuss the subject of manufacturers' catalogs and their historical as well as practical value to the profession of librarianship. Dr. Mount has made an outstanding contribution." (Academic Library Book Review)*

Role of Standards in Sci-Tech Libraries, edited by Ellis Mount, DLS (Vol. 10, No. 3, 1990). *Required reading for any librarian who has been asked to identify standards and specifications.*

Relation of Sci-Tech Information to Environmental Studies, edited by Ellis Mount, DLS (Vol. 10, No. 2, 1990). *"A timely and important book that illustrates the nature and use of sci-tech information in relation to the environment." (The Bulletin of Science, Technology & Society)*

End-User Training for Sci-Tech Databases, edited by Ellis Mount, DLS (Vol. 10, No. 1, 1990). *"This is a timely publication for those of us involved in conducting online searches in special libraries where our users have a detailed knowledge of their subject areas." (Australian Library Review)*

Sci-Tech Archives and Manuscript Collections, edited by Ellis Mount, DLS (Vol. 9, No. 4, 1989). *Gain valuable information on the ways in which sci-tech archival material is being handled and preserved in various institutions and organizations.*

Collection Management in Sci-Tech Libraries, edited by Ellis Mount, DLS (Vol. 9, No. 3, 1989). *"An interesting and timely survey of current issues in collection management as they pertain to science and technology libraries." (Barbara A. List, AMLS, Coordinator of Collection Development, Science & Technology Research Center, and Editor, New Technical Books, The Research Libraries, New York Public Library)*

The Role of Conference Literature in Sci-Tech Libraries, edited by Ellis Mount, DLS (Vol. 9, No. 2, 1989). *"The volume constitutes a valuable overview of the issues posed for librarians and users by one of the most frustrating and yet important sources of scientific and technical information." (Australian Library Review)*

Adaptation of Turnkey Computer Systems in Sci-Tech Libraries, edited by Ellis Mount, DLS (Vol. 9, No. 1, 1989). *"Interesting and useful. . . . The book addresses the problems and benefits associated with the installation of a turnkey or ready-made computer system in a scientific or technical library." (Information Retrieval & Library Automation)*

Sci-Tech Libraries Serving Zoological Gardens, edited by Ellis Mount, DLS (Vol. 8, No. 4, 1989). *"Reviews the history and development of six major zoological garden libraries in the U.S." (Australian Library Review)*

Libraries Serving Science-Oriented and Vocational High Schools, edited by Ellis Mount, DLS (Vol. 8, No. 3, 1989). *A wealth of information on the special collections of science-oriented and vocational high schools, with a look at their services, students, activities, and problems.*

Sci-Tech Library Networks Within Organizations, edited by Ellis Mount, DLS (Vol. 8, No. 2, 1988). *Offers thorough descriptions of sci-tech library networks in which their members have a common sponsorship or ownership.*

One Hundred Years of Sci-Tech Libraries: A Brief History, edited by Ellis Mount, DLS (Vol. 8, No. 1, 1988). *"Should be read by all those considering, or who are already involved in, information retrieval, whether in Sci-tech libraries or others." (Library Resources & Technical Services)*

Alternative Careers in Sci-Tech Information Service, edited by Ellis Mount, DLS (Vol. 7, No. 4, 1987). *Here is an eye-opening look at alternative careers for professionals with a sci-tech background, including librarians, scientists, and engineers.*

Preservation and Conservation of Sci-Tech Materials, edited by Ellis Mount, DLS (Vol. 7, No. 3, 1987). *"This cleverly coordinated work is essential reading for library school students and practicing librarians. . . . Recommended reading." (Science Books and Films)*

Sci-Tech Libraries Serving Societies and Institutions, edited by Ellis Mount, DLS (Vol. 7, No. 2, 1987). *"Of most interest to special librarians, providing them with some insight into sci-tech libraries and their activities as well as a means of identifying specialized services and collections which may be of use to them." (Sci-Tech Libraries)*

Innovations in Planning Facilities for Sci-Tech Libraries, edited by Ellis Mount, DLS (Vol. 7, No. 1, 1986). *"Will prove invaluable to any librarian establishing a new library or contemplating expansion." (Australasian College Libraries)*

Role of Computers in Sci-Tech Libraries, edited by Ellis Mount, DLS (Vol. 6, No. 4, 1986). *"A very readable text. . . . I am including a number of the articles in the student reading list." (C. Bull, Kingstec Community College, Kentville, Nova Scotia, Canada)*

Weeding of Collections in Sci-Tech Libraries, edited by Ellis Mount, DLS (Vol. 6, No. 3, 1986). *"A useful publication. . . . Should be in every science and technology library." (Rivernia Library Review)*

Sci-Tech Libraries in Museums and Aquariums, edited by Ellis Mount, DLS (Vol. 6, No. 1/2, 1985). *"Useful to libraries in museums and aquariums for its descriptive and practical information." (The Association for Information Management)*

Data Manipulation in Sci-Tech Libraries, edited by Ellis Mount, DLS (Vol. 5, No. 4, 1985). *"Papers in this volume present evidence of the growing sophistication in the manipulation of data by information personnel." (Sci-Tech Book News)*

Role of Maps in Sci-Tech Libraries, edited by Ellis Mount, DLS (Vol. 5, No. 3, 1985). *Learn all about the acquisition of maps and the special problems of their storage and preservation in this insightful book.*

Fee-Based Services in Sci-Tech Libraries, edited by Ellis Mount, DLS (Vol. 5, No. 2, 1985). *"Highly recommended. Any librarian will find something of interest in this volume." (Australasian College Libraries)*

Serving End-Users in Sci-Tech Libraries, edited by Ellis Mount, DLS (Vol. 5, No. 1, 1984). *"Welcome and indeed interesting reading. . . . a useful acquisition for anyone starting out in one or more of the areas covered." (Australasian College Libraries)*

Management of Sci-Tech Libraries, edited by Ellis Mount, DLS (Vol. 4, No. 3/4, 1984). *Become better equipped to tackle difficult staffing, budgeting, and personnel challenges with this essential volume on managing different types of sci-tech libraries.*

Collection Development in Sci-Tech Libraries, edited by Ellis Mount, DLS (Vol. 4, No. 2, 1984). *"Well-written by authors who work in the field they are discussing. Should be of value to librarians whose collections cover a wide range of scientific and technical fields." (Library Acquisitions: Practice and Theory)*

Role of Serials in Sci-Tech Libraries, edited by Ellis Mount, DLS (Vol. 4, No. 1, 1983). *"Some interesting nuggets to offer dedicated serials librarians and users of scientific journal literature. . . . Outlines the direction of some major changes already occurring in scientific journal publishing and serials management." (Serials Review)*

Planning Facilities for Sci-Tech Libraries, edited by Ellis Mount, DLS (Vol. 3, No. 4, 1983). *"Will be of interest to special librarians who are contemplating the building of new facilities or the renovating and adaptation of existing facilities in the near future. . . . A useful manual based on actual experiences." (Sci-Tech News)*

Monographs in Sci-Tech Libraries, edited by Ellis Mount, DLS (Vol. 3, No. 3, 1983). *This insightful book addresses the present contributions monographs are making in sci-tech libraries as well as their probable role in the future.*

Role of Translations in Sci-Tech Libraries, edited by Ellis Mount, DLS (Vol. 3, No. 2, 1983). *"Good required reading in a course on special libraries in library school. It would also be useful to any librarian who handles the ordering of translations." (Sci-Tech News)*

Online versus Manual Searching in Sci-Tech Libraries, edited by Ellis Mount, DLS (Vol. 3, No. 1, 1982). *An authoritative volume that examines the role that manual searches play in academic, public, corporate, and hospital libraries.*

Document Delivery for Sci-Tech Libraries, edited by Ellis Mount, DLS (Vol. 2, No. 4, 1982). *Touches on important aspects of document delivery and the place each aspect holds in the overall scheme of things.*

Cataloging and Indexing for Sci-Tech Libraries, edited by Ellis Mount, DLS (Vol. 2, No. 3, 1982). *Diverse and authoritative views on the problems of cataloging and indexing in sci-tech libraries.*

Role of Patents in Sci-Tech Libraries, edited by Ellis Mount, DLS (Vol. 2, No. 2, 1982). *A fascinating look at the nature of patents and the complicated, ever-changing set of indexes and computerized databases devoted to facilitating the identification and retrieval of patents.*

Current Awareness Services in Sci-Tech Libraries, edited by Ellis Mount, DLS (Vol. 2, No. 1, 1982). *An interesting and comprehensive look at the many forms of current awareness services that sci-tech libraries offer.*

Role of Technical Reports in Sci-Tech Libraries, edited by Ellis Mount, DLS (Vol. 1, No. 4, 1982). *Recommended reading not only for science and technology librarians, this unique volume is specifically devoted to the analysis of problems, innovative practices, and advances relating to the control and servicing of technical reports.*

Training of Sci-Tech Librarians and Library Users, edited by Ellis Mount, DLS (Vol. 1, No. 3, 1981). *Here is a crucial overview of the current and future issues in the training of science and engineering librarians as well as instruction for users of these libraries.*

Networking in Sci-Tech Libraries and Information Centers, edited by Ellis Mount, DLS (Vol. 1, No. 2, 1981). *Here is an entire volume devoted to the topic of cooperative projects and library networks among sci-tech libraries.*

Planning for Online Search Service in Sci-Tech Libraries, edited by Ellis Mount, DLS (Vol. 1, No. 1, 1981). *Covers the most important issue to consider when planning for online search services.*

Online Ecological
and Environmental Data

Virginia Baldwin
Editor

Online Ecological and Environmental Data has been co-published simultaneously as *Science & Technology Libraries*, Volume 23, Number 4 2003.

Routledge
Taylor & Francis Group

LONDON AND NEW YORK

First published 2003 by The Haworth Information Press®

2 Park Square, Milton Park, Abingdon, Oxfordshire OX14 4RN
605 Third Avenue, New York, NY 10017

Routledge is an imprint of the Taylor & Francis Group, an informa business

First issued in paperback 2020

Online Ecological and Environmental Data has been co-published simultaneously as *Science & Technology Libraries*™, Volume 23, Number 4 2003.

Cover design by Lora Wiggins.

Library of Congress Cataloging-in-Publication Data

Online ecological and environmental data / Virginia Baldwin, editor.
     p. cm.
     "Co-published simultaneously as Science & technology libraries, volume 23, number 4."
     Includes bibliographical references and index.
     ISBN 0-7890-2446-2 (alk. paper) – ISBN 0-7890-2447-0 (pbk. : alk. paper)
     1. Environmental sciences–Computer network resources. 2. Environmental sciences–Databases. I. Baldwin, Virginia A. II. Science & technology libraries.
GE32.O55 2004
025.06'33372–dc22

                                     2003027494

ISBN : 978-0-7890-2446-6 (hbk)
ISBN : 978-0-7890-2447-3 (pbk)

Indexing, Abstracting & Website/Internet Coverage

Science & Technology Libraries

This section provides you with a list of major indexing & abstracting services. That is to say, each service began covering this periodical during the year noted in the right column. Most Websites which are listed below have indicated that they will either post, disseminate, compile, archive, cite or alert their own Website users with research-based content from this work. (This list is as current as the copyright date of this publication.)

Abstracting, Website/Indexing Coverage . . . . Year When Coverage Began

- *AGRICOLA Database (AGRICultural OnLine Access): A Bibliographic database of citations to the agricultural literature created by the National Agricultural Library and its cooperators* <http://www.natl.usda.gov/ag98> 1989

- *AGRIS* 1989

- *Aluminum Industry Abstracts* <http://www.csa.com> 2003

- *Biosciences Information Service of Biological Abstracts (BIOSIS) a centralized source of life science information* <http://www.biosis.org>. 1982

- *BIOSIS Previews: online version of Biological Abstracts and Biological Abstracts/RRM (Reports, Reviews, Meetings); Covers approximately 6,500 life science journals and 2,000 worldwide meetings* 1982

- *Cambridge Scientific Abstracts is a leading publisher of scientific information in print journals, online databases, CD-ROM and via the Internet* <http://www.csa.com> 2003

- *Ceramic Abstracts* <http://www.csa.com>. 2003

- *Chemical Abstracts Service–monitors, indexes & abstracts the world's chemical literature, updates this information daily, and makes it accessible through state-of-the-art information services* <http://www.cas.org> 1989

(continued)

(continued)

*Exact start date to come.

(continued)

*Special Bibliographic Notes related to special journal issues
(separates) and indexing/abstracting:*

- indexing/abstracting services in this list will also cover material in any "separate" that is co-published simultaneously with Haworth's special thematic journal issue or DocuSerial. Indexing/abstracting usually covers material at the article/chapter level.
- monographic co-editions are intended for either non-subscribers or libraries which intend to purchase a second copy for their circulating collections.
- monographic co-editions are reported to all jobbers/wholesalers/approval plans. The source journal is listed as the "series" to assist the prevention of duplicate purchasing in the same manner utilized for books-in-series.
- to facilitate user/access services all indexing/abstracting services are encouraged to utilize the co-indexing entry note indicated at the bottom of the first page of each article/chapter/contribution.
- this is intended to assist a library user of any reference tool (whether print, electronic, online, or CD-ROM) to locate the monographic version if the library has purchased this version but not a subscription to the source journal.
- individual articles/chapters in any Haworth publication are also available through the Haworth Document Delivery Service (HDDS).

Online Ecological and Environmental Data

CONTENTS

ABOUT THE EDITOR

Virginia (Ginny) Baldwin, BS, MS, MLS, is Professor and Head of the Engineering Library, and the Physics and Astronomy Librarian at the University of Nebraska in Lincoln. Ms. Baldwin is also the Patent and Trademark Librarian for the State of Nebraska. She is a former Scientific Programmer at Patrick Air Force Base in Florida, and an Engineer Specialist at Vandenberg Air Force Base in California. For nine years at Eastern Illinois University, she was responsible for collection development and specialized reference and library instruction in the engineering, computer science, and physical science disciplines. She was awarded academic tenure at Eastern Illinois University in 1997 and promoted to Professor in 1999.

Ms. Baldwin is the Editor of *Science & Technology Libraries*. She has been published in several journals, including *College and Research Libraries*, *Collection Management*, *Illinois Libraries*, *Journal of Technology Studies*, and *To Improve the Academy*, the Annual of the Professional and Organizational Development Network in Higher Education. She also authored a chapter in *Electronic Collection Management* (The Haworth Press, Inc.). She is the liaison from the Sci-Tech Division of Special Libraries Association to the Sci-Tech Section of the Association of College and Research Libraries, and is a member of both associations. Ms. Baldwin is also a member of the American Society for Engineering Education.

Introduction

The advent of the Internet and proliferation of materials on it has brought significant and rapid change in scholarly communication. Perhaps more gradually has come the posting of research data for sharing with other researchers in the field. This volume describes several projects that have made environmental and ecological researchers' data freely available online. Librarians from the National Aeronautics and Space Administration (NASA), the United States Geological Survey (USGS), from one regional agency based in Oregon, one university, and one research corporation describe aspects of the online data projects developed by their respective institutions. A sixth paper, from a librarian at State University of New York University at Buffalo, follows the development of online research data in a specific field, acid rain research, from a variety of types of research programs. A common theme in these papers is the interdisciplinary involvement of researchers who produce and use data in the fields of environmental and ecological studies.

In their paper, "Cooperative Design, Development, and Management of Interdisciplinary Data to Support the Global Environmental Change Research Community," Downs and Chen taut the value of online data for interdisciplinary research while calling our attention to the principally unrecognized difficulties due to differences in the terminology and protocols of various disciplines and the ability to interpret the meaning of data gathered for the research in another discipline. Described in this paper are a multitude of factors that required definition, structure, and procedures to develop the Center for International Earth Science Information Network (CIESIN) at Columbia University. Here an organizational system and administrative infrastructure of knowledge workers and information systems was developed to foster and support interdisciplinary research that is focused on global environmental change (GEC). This is an appropriate opening for this volume as it lays the foundation for the various aspects for consideration in such projects. For example, the authors describe in detail processes involving

[Haworth co-indexing entry note]: "Introduction." Baldwin, Virginia. Co-published simultaneously in *Science & Technology Libraries* (The Haworth Information Press, an imprint of The Haworth Press, Inc.) Vol. 23, No. 4, 2003, pp. 1-4; and: *Online Ecological and Environmental Data* (ed: Virginia Baldwin) The Haworth Information Press, an imprint of The Haworth Press, Inc., 2003, pp. 1-4. Single or multiple copies of this article are available for a fee from The Haworth Document Delivery Service [1-800-HAWORTH, 9:00 a.m. - 5:00 p.m. (EST). E-mail address: docdelivery@haworthpress.com].

Digital Object Identifier: 10.1300/J122v23n04_01

intellectual property rights management, identification of qualifying data to be included and acquired, internal cataloging, the establishment of metadata (essentially data about data) criteria, web designers and other professionals to facilitate access to the varied user community, archiving considerations, and facilitation of identification and assistance with retrieval of needed resources by the user community. Qualifying data for inclusion involves a peer review process similar to that used for journal publication. Quantitative metrics are collected to assess viability of the data center, data delivery, and user satisfaction. In the article, sample online data products are described as well as future project directions and ongoing partnerships.

A government agency interdisciplinary online data project is described in "Beyond Bibliography: A Dynamic Approach to the Cataloging of Multidisciplinary Environmental Data for Global Change Research." Gene R. Major describes the multidisciplinary field of global environmental change research as being comprised of oceanographers, climatologists, ecologists, geologists, hydrologists, agriculture researchers, geophysicists, and health researchers, among others. In this paper, Major describes in detail the challenges of developing and applying new technologies of adapting research data for online interdisciplinary research use and for sharing metadata. Keys to aid researchers and librarians in locating the data in the NASA database, Global Change Master Directory (GCMD), are the hierarchical structure of the controlled vocabularies that describe the earth science data sets in the Directory and the use of semantic metadata in a particular format (Directory Interchange Format (DIF)). In many disciplines the researcher's data often vanishes once the analysis is done and the paper published. As with many other fields, preservation of global change research data is important to advance the understanding of this area of vital importance.

While the first two papers in this volume provide detailed insight into some of the management principles and concepts involved in universal access into online data, in his paper, "A National Environmental Data Network Revealed Through the Study of Acid Rain," Fred Stoss tracks the availability of research data for one particular global environmental problem, that of acid rain. Of especial interest in this paper is the historical perspective that contributed to the building of acid rain information from decades of research, and the subsequent development of online access to environmental and ecological data from these studies. Stoss also describes representative samples from a variety of government agencies, universities, and organizations that provide data related to acid rain research and related studies, and outlines future prospects for the development, recognition, and use of these online sources of data.

The fourth paper, "Information Science and Technology Developments Within the National Biological Information Infrastructure" describes a portal project for specific biological collections available on the Web. Created by a federal government agency, the USGS, the National Biological Information Infrastructure (NBII) is the nation's biological portal to all biological data and information within the United States, and is the United States's contribution to several international initiatives. In this paper, four co-authors from two different USGS agencies describe the challenges of the biological information world and the program, NBII, which was developed to address the challenges on a national scale. The portal, BioBot, is an intelligent agent that targets the NBII collection, major search engines and indexes, and specific biological collections on the Web. The accompanying profiling capability for current awareness, thesaurus structure, an individual user portal (NBII Knowledge portal), and the use of metatags are important features of this program. Also described is a public/private partnership with CSA, a publisher of indexes and abstracts for scientific literature for over thirty years, to provide a freely available single dissemination point for biocomplexity information from proprietary and nonproprietary (Web) resources.

In "Syracuse Research Corporation's Chemical Information Databases: Extraction and Compilation of Data Related to Environmental Fate and Exposure" seven co-authors from the Syracuse Research Corporation describe another government/private sector partnership. In a project sponsored by the Environmental Protection Agency, data related to the health and environmental impacts of chemicals are extracted from research publications, bibliographically referenced, and made available through several databases produced and maintained by Syracuse Research Corporation. Other databases that provide environmentally relevant physical and test properties and actual data files are completely accessible to the public. Licensed commercial PC versions provide enhancements to the interface.

The final article, "Convergence and Dissemination: A Brief History and Description of the StreamNet Project" is significant in that it portrays the development of a portal through which various researchers in the region deposit and disseminate information on fish and fisheries for the entire Columbia Basin Fish and Wildlife Program. StreamNet Regional Librarian, Lenora A. Oftedahl, describes the StreamNet Project and the StreamNet Library that archives and makes accessible the regional data and the referenced documents.

Further studies to identify fields of study in which actual research data is being shared online would be valuable to researchers, librarians, and their clients. Certainly the projects described in this volume serve as models for other disciplines, especially for the various aspects of handling data made available online, and for the structures of controlled vocabulary and metadata that make this data more accessible and usable on the Internet.

ACKNOWLEDGEMENT

The editor expresses gratitude for identifying and soliciting manuscripts from the authors of this thematic issue to Fred Stoss, an Associate Librarian in the Science and Engineering Library at the State University of New York University at Buffalo. Stoss holds Master of Science Degrees in zoology and in library science and has worked at the Center for Environmental Information, the Energy, Environment, and Resources Center of the University of Tennessee in Knoxville and at Oak Ridge National Laboratory.

Virginia Baldwin
Editor

Cooperative Design, Development, and Management of Interdisciplinary Data to Support the Global Environmental Change Research Community

Robert R. Downs
Robert S. Chen

SUMMARY. This article describes the organizational, collaborative, and project management processes of a scientific data center that serves the interdisciplinary global environmental change research community. Collaborating with representatives of the user community, the data center identifies, acquires, ingests, manages, and disseminates research-related information (RRI), such as scientific data and documents. Users and software developers cooperatively design online applications that integrate these resources into a wide variety of information products and services to be disseminated through a digital library to the globally dispersed community. Results from these participatory design and cooperative development activities include

Robert R. Downs, PhD, is Senior Digital Archivist and Robert S. Chen, PhD, is Deputy Director and Senior Research Scientist, both at the Center for International Earth Science Information Network (CIESIN) of Columbia University.

The authors acknowledge support from the NASA Socioeconomic Data and Applications Center (SEDAC) under contract NAS5-98162.

The opinions expressed here are those of the authors and are not necessarily the viewpoints of CIESIN, Columbia University, or NASA.

[Haworth co-indexing entry note]: "Cooperative Design, Development, and Management of Interdisciplinary Data to Support the Global Environmental Change Research Community." Downs, Robert R., and Robert S. Chen. Co-published simultaneously in *Science & Technology Libraries* (The Haworth Information Press, an imprint of The Haworth Press, Inc.) Vol. 23, No. 4, 2003, pp. 5-19; and: *Online Ecological and Environmental Data* (ed: Virginia Baldwin) The Haworth Information Press, an imprint of The Haworth Press, Inc., 2003, pp. 5-19. Single or multiple copies of this article are available for a fee from The Haworth Document Delivery Service [1-800-HAWORTH, 9:00 a.m. - 5:00 p.m. (EST). E-mail address: docdelivery@haworthpress.com].

Web-based resource catalogs, training, peer education, help desk, and reference services to support scientific communication and decision-making among members of the interdisciplinary community. *[Article copies available for a fee from The Haworth Document Delivery Service: 1-800-HAWORTH. E-mail address: <docdelivery@haworthpress.com> Website: <http://www.Haworth Press.com> © 2003 by The Haworth Press, Inc. All rights reserved.]*

KEYWORDS. Data center, digital library, participatory design, interdisciplinary research, user community, research-related information, earth science data, scientific communities, collaborative development

INTRODUCTION

Sharing data, documents, and other research-related information (RRI) within the research community is central to the scientific process. In addition to reading results in journals representing their respective disciplines, researchers need to study data, procedures, instruments, notes, and other descriptive information to replicate and build on the research of others. Computing and communication technologies now enable processing of RRI to develop products and services for dissemination to support the decision-making and research activities of globally dispersed scientific communities. The use of these technologies is changing the practices and models of scientific communication (Hurd, 2000). The online availability of data products and services representing different disciplines also contributes to the capabilities available for conducting interdisciplinary research, enabling scientists to expand beyond their own disciplines to share their data and documents with others who may approach problems from different perspectives. Although it may be difficult to understand the terminology and protocols of other scientific disciplines, interdisciplinary research efforts can identify and explore relationships in data that might otherwise be difficult to observe from a single discipline.

Supporting interdisciplinary research requires the establishment of capabilities to analyze data from different scientific disciplines of interest. Interdisciplinary research also requires an understanding of the meaning of data that comes from other disciplines (Chen, 1981). Describing RRI provided by scientists from distinct disciplines and developing products and services to support interdisciplinary research effectively requires cooperation among data providers, data centers, and users. However, such cooperative design and development efforts require organizational, social, and project management processes to coordinate interdisciplinary teams of collaborators. Organizational coordination also is required to develop and maintain online applications that foster interactive access, visualization, and analysis of data. Facilitating online analysis of information interactively requires an administrative infrastructure of knowledge workers and information systems (McGlamery, 1999). The Center for International Earth Science Information Network (CIESIN) of Columbia University has developed and organized a data center to meet these challenges, focusing specifically on global environmental change (GEC) and associated human interactions.

Recognition of the significance of GEC and its potential implications for human activities and welfare has grown substantially during the past three decades. During this time, a large, globally distributed community of natural and social scientists has emerged who are concerned with a diverse set of issues associated with global change, ranging from short-term environmental variability to long-term changes in the Earth's climate. In particular, this community has extensively documented the many different ways in which human activities and social organization affect and are affected by environmental processes from local to global scales. This has led to the recognition of the importance of environmental sustainability–encompassing both human and environmental systems and a range of spatial and temporal scales–and the identification of the need for a corresponding interdisciplinary "sustainability science" (Kates et al., 2001; NRC, 2000).

In an effort to advance understanding of human interactions in the environment, CIESIN works closely with the interdisciplinary GEC research community to support the use of scientific data and other RRI. Through its cooperative design, development, and management processes, CIESIN fosters such collaboration among stakeholders to support decision-making, research, and educational activities. Established as a consortium in Michigan in 1989, CIESIN became a center of Columbia University's Earth Institute in 1998. CIESIN archives data and other RRI, integrates these into its Web-based systems to develop interactive products and services, and provides continuing support of their use by patrons within the stakeholder community. The community primarily consists of faculty, researchers, students, librarians, resource developers, and public and private decision-makers who have an interest in understanding human interactions in the environment. Community members represent various educational disciplines including the earth, environmental, health, and social sciences in primary, secondary, higher education, and in research institutions. They also represent government and non-profit organizations.

CIESIN manages several programs and projects to serve its community of stakeholders. CIESIN operates the Socioeconomic Data and Applications Center (SEDAC) for the U.S. National Aeronautics and Space Administration (NASA) Earth Observing System Data Information System. It also hosts the Global Change Research Information Office (GCRIO) for the U.S. Global Change Research Program and has been designated the World Data Center for

Human Interactions in the Environment by the International Council of Science (ICSU). In addition, various projects are conducted with Columbia University partners and other organizations to investigate, advance, and promote understanding of human interactions in the environment.

CIESIN actively develops and sustains an online archive, or digital library, to disseminate data and other RRI along with products derived from these resources and services to support the user community. The data center archives and disseminates original resources from data providers and value-added information products developed by the data center and its partners. Data Center services include preserving, organizing, describing, and integrating the resources into its digital library and supporting their use to facilitate discovery, access, learning, analysis, and extraction by members of the global change research community.

CIESIN has been building a variety of processes to coordinate the efforts of its programs and projects that support understanding on interactions in the environment. In addition to cooperative design, development, and project management activities of the data center, there are a variety of processes associated with operating the digital library, maintaining the products and services, and supporting scientific communication and decision-making activities conducted by members of the community. All of these organizational, project, and data management processes contribute to the virtual infrastructure that enables the data center to develop and sustain the information products and services that it provides for the research community.

COOPERATIVE PROCESSES

Data center staff and community members collaboratively employ a user-centered approach to develop interactive applications from interdisciplinary data. In addition, the center develops policies to inform the development of plans, procedures, processes, and practices to foster data stewardship and the development of products and services to study human interactions in the environment.

The processes completed by CIESIN to produce products and services include activities to initiate a project, such as requirements planning, proposing funding, and identifying RRI and other information resources for potential use; nominating data or other RRI for acquisition; procuring intellectual property permissions; internal cataloging, ingest of original RRI, preservation, and preparation of descriptive information; design, development, testing, and review; and product archiving, online cataloging and reference services.

CIESIN scientists and professionals, representing various disciplines, are organized within a matrix organizational structure. This structure combines a functional reporting framework with individual project management requirements to meet the information and data management needs of a data center that simultaneously sustains diverse digital archiving, Web-based product development, and community support services.

The functional reporting framework of the center consists of three work groups, labeled information technology, information services, and science applications. The information technology work group includes computer scientists and information system professionals experienced in designing, developing, and supporting Web-based information retrieval systems and database management systems. The information services group consists of information scientists and information management professionals experienced in digital preservation, cataloging, and providing reference consulting. The science applications group includes scientists from fields within the natural, social, and health sciences, and professionals with expertise in geographic information systems and remote sensing.

Specific projects are initiated in cooperation with the community of stakeholders after an opportunity has been identified to resolve a research problem or decision-making need. Identifying project opportunities involves continuing communications with partners and collaborators on their ongoing research activities as well as close monitoring of evolving technologies. One way of accomplishing this goal is to organize meetings, workshops, conferences, and online discussion groups that bring together scientists and decision-makers within the global change research community to focus on topics of interest. CIESIN has sponsored or cosponsored a number of user workshops on topics ranging from international environmental treaties to gridding of population data, and also hosts a number of online discussion lists and resources. Data center staff members actively participate in these activities and in discussion groups, forums, and events sponsored by the scientific and professional organizations in which they belong. Ideas for research projects often emerge during these activities. Individuals with common interests meet to discuss issues and form groups to organize those who can participate in related activities.

Data center involvement in an initiative is contingent upon recognition of the value of potential results and the identification of organizational resources that can contribute to the successful completion of the project. It is important to identify the purpose, the availability of appropriate expertise, the existence of needed capabilities and resources, and an individual who will lead the project. The purpose of the initiative must be compatible with the mission and current strategies of the data center.

A data center staff member is needed to coordinate project activities, request resources, and ensure that it meets the objectives. Acting as the champion for the project, the project leader proposes, guides, and nurtures the project through the various processes necessary to insure its successful completion. The project leader establishes a team of data center staff and members of the community who coordinate their efforts to complete the project.

Initial planning meetings facilitate coordination by enabling ideas and concerns to be documented. The evolving plans initially identify project objectives, potential user groups and expected benefits to them, source of funding and types of resources needed (human, data, infrastructure, information, materials) and their potential costs as well as the constraints (schedule, available funding). Human resources include a schedule of internal staff requirements, along with efforts required from partners and collaborators. As requirements and resources are specified, assignments and schedules can be created and subsequently refined. Successive meetings of team members foster continual planning and development throughout the project to ensure that the objectives will be achieved.

PROJECT INITIATION

Research resources that could contribute to an initiative must be identified early in the project. Scientists on staff and within the user community who are familiar with current research activities participate in this effort by suggesting potential resources to be nominated for a project.

The process of identifying and qualifying data and documents for inclusion in the online archive includes review of the published research results that already have been subjected to the rigorous review that is associated with the editorial practices of the scientific publications in their respective fields. Similar to the review process in publishing reports of research results, the nominated RRI, consisting of data and documents, also are refereed by members of the scientific community to qualify for processing by the data center. In the case of SEDAC, a standing external advisory committee, the SEDAC User Working Group (UWG), fulfills this role. The UWG, which currently includes 18 individuals drawn from the natural, social, and computer sciences and from several applications areas (http://sedac.ciesin.columbia.edu/contact.html), meets twice yearly to review SEDAC project plans and approve key data for dissemination. Approval resulting from peer reviews by the scientific community triggers a host of library and information processing activities resulting in the development and dissemination of data products and information services to scientific, educational, and decision-making communities worldwide.

ACQUISITION AND INITIAL ARCHIVING PROCESSES

Once approved by the referees representing the scientific community of users, the data and other RRI must be acquired by the data center. Acquisition involves negotiating the intellectual property rights to be obtained from the owner and procuring the original resources and relevant supporting documentation from the owner and/or other parties.

Intellectual property rights management facilitates recognition and documentation of the role of authors and data providers who contributed to the creation of the data sets, instruments, and the related resources. Negotiations for intellectual property permissions begin informally when the team is considering data, documents, or other RRI for nomination to a collection. Although copyright and permissions statements are often displayed on Web sites, McCain (2000) found that more than half (54%) of the data providers observed did not publicize on their Web pages, any statement regarding intellectual property permissions for accessing, using, or disseminating the RRI provided. When available, such statements can provide the user with an indication of the intellectual property rights granted to the data center and to third-party users. For digital rights management, CIESIN has created standard forms with advice from legal counsel, to facilitate obtaining written authorization from owners for using and disseminating specific resources. For more complex negotiations, either a memorandum of understanding or a separate contract between both parties is created, specifying the rights and obligations of each party.

In most cases the resources are in digital form and do not require digitization. However, the original resources must be identified along with documents describing them, inventoried, and transferred to the data center, which can require assistance from the creators. Once intellectual property permissions, original resources, and supporting materials are acquired, digital archiving of the acquired resources, including internal cataloging and ingest, can be completed.

Internal cataloging efforts describe each resource to facilitate record mangement, document tracking, digital preservation, and data management. Items initially collected for internal cataloging include the permissions documents and the documentation initially obtained by the scientist to determine the applicability of a resource for the project. The digital archivist analyzes these data and documents to create an internal catalog record containing the preservation, structural, and administrative metadata describing the original resource. When the documents obtained do not contain all of the descriptive information that is needed for internal cataloging, the resource provider is contacted to request additional information. Once an original resource has been described in the internal catalog, the resource, along with its preservation information and supporting documentation, is prepared for ingest.

Working with the project leader and the scientist most familiar with a particular resource, the digital archivist identifies, inventories, collects, inspects, tests, and prepares the original resources, the supporting materials, and the administrative and preservation information for ingest. The digital materials are stored online for access by the design and development team and housed off-line on CD-R media in two separate archives. For immediate accessibility, archived media are housed on site at CIESIN's primary facility. In cooperation with a research center at another location, CIESIN maintains a duplicate archive off-site to facilitate recovery in the event of a disaster at the data center.

DESIGN AND DEVELOPMENT PROCESSES

A team of scientists, Web-designers, and programmers create a data applications development plan to coordinate the design and development of the products and services that will facilitate access and use of the RRI. This design team coordinates the design and development of the information products and services, articulating various user scenarios to demonstrate how users will interact with data and services. Members of the team then identify or design the software that will disseminate the resource, and develop the programs and user interfaces to facilitate access and use. Other data center staff and members of the community also participate in various aspects of this iterative design and development process. Such activities often include converting the original resources into standard formats and integrating them into a specific dissemination system to promote interactive discovery, access, analysis, presentation, and extraction by individuals from the user community.

Working with managers of the data center, the team creates a schedule based on the availability of staff needed for the design and development effort. The design team establishes the initial design requirements from concepts, scenarios, and expectations that the scientists present for accessing and using the resources. CIESIN scientists present the development plan, initial concepts, and mock-up designs to scientists within the community and other stakeholders for comment. Based on these reviews, the identified requirements evolve and successive revisions are presented initially as mock-ups and subsequently, as early prototypes, to all data center staff with a request for comments. In effect, the design requirements emerge as designers and users construct a model that meets their shared and evolving understanding of how the new services can meet their needs.

The service is modified iteratively, based on ensuing reviews, in "alpha" and "beta" test environments before it can be published in a production system. Members of the user community are invited to comment on the design and participate more actively in the development of products and services (Downs, 2001). For SEDAC data and services, a configuration management board (CMB), consisting of SEDAC managers, scientists, and task leaders, must approve the development and dissemination plan for any proposed additions or changes before they are implemented on either the beta test system or the production system. This formal review process is part of the change management procedure to ensure that all usability and security requirements are met before new products or services are integrated with other resources residing on the systems.

Completed information systems, applications, and products also must be archived to facilitate recovery and foster subsequent development efforts. Based on the evolving development and dissemination plan, the project leader, digital archivists, domain scientists, and development professionals create an archiving plan for the new product and its related services. In addition to the original resources initially ingested, objects identified for archiving include the value-added data produced at the data center, the programs used for intermediate processing, and the resulting information products and presentation programs. Similar to the original resources, archived products are stored on CD-R media and housed within the center and off-site at a cooperating center.

The project leader, participating scientists, developers, and digital archivists assist the online cataloging staff in describing the Web-based products to facilitate their promotion, discovery, and use. The cataloging staff describes the products, complying with the Federal Geographic Data Committee (FGDC) Content Standard for Digital Geospatial Metadata (CSDGM) and NASA formats including the Directory Interchange Format (DIF). Descriptions of CIESIN products and descriptions of related products disseminated by other data centers are published in the SEDAC Information Gateway catalog, an online finding aid for resources related to human interactions in the environment. Catalogers also provide spatial metadata training for staff in other data centers to assist them in improving their cataloging capabilities.

DISSEMINATION AND SUPPORT PROCESSES

These activities have produced a wide array of information products and services to support the user community. Online services support a variety of navigation capabilities and multiple data protocols for extraction. They are designed to enable interactive discovery, access, and analysis by globally distributed community members representing diverse backgrounds, disciplines, and levels of expertise. Advanced features offer opportunities for researchers, scientists, and decision-makers to more precisely specify values for selecting and analyzing data. Alternatively, educators and students can use simple user interface features to explore topics of interest before examining specific issues or requesting specific datasets.

In an effort to facilitate discovery, the online products and services are presented within organized categories on the CIESIN Web site to assist community members in identifying and selecting resources. Users may Browse by

Subject, choose Online Tools and Applications, find Downloadable Data, or search Metadata Catalogs.

Cooperation among staff and community members enables reference consultants to assist the community on their use of resources offered by CIESIN and in their understanding of human interactions in the environment. Community members receive answers to their questions by calling on the telephone, submitting inquiries by electronic or paper mail, or searching an interactive database of questions. An interdisciplinary intermediary staff provides first-line support of the multi-tiered reference service, answering the majority of reference questions received or providing referrals to other pertinent reference services.

Messages requiring specific expertise are forwarded to the appropriate work groups to provide accurate and timely responses to requests. Reference intermediaries send questions requiring scientific expertise to the available scientist who possesses the requisite knowledge or to all staff if an expert cannot be identified. Any new questions and answers are added to a reference database that is maintained to support interactive Web-based queries that are posed by community members. Community members also ask system-related questions, notify reference services staff about system failures experienced, and offer suggestions for improving the interface, the quality, or the functionality of products and services offered. Messages about the system performance are forwarded to the system support group.

In addition to cooperating with the reference consultants and the user community to maintain the systems and improve server response time, system engineers collaborate with scientists to identify potential needs and future system capabilities. Likewise, scientists discuss their plans regarding collection development with the systems administrators so that system enhancements and upgrades can be scheduled to meet changes in demand.

An area of increasing effort is the production of quantitative "metrics" to assess how well the data center is doing in terms of data delivery and user satisfaction. Current metrics being collected by SEDAC include data volume, error rates, favorable/unfavorable user comments, and a simple user satisfaction survey. Unfortunately, these quantitative metrics do not clearly match the basic objective of the data center, to support interdisciplinary research. More qualitative measures, such as the use of data in peer-reviewed research or comments by external reviewers, advisors, and users, continue to be important sources of input into data center planning and operations.

EXAMPLE PRODUCTS AND SERVICES

A few examples of CIESIN-developed data and other RRI can illustrate the outcomes of CIESIN's cooperative processes.

Gridded Population of the World (GPW)

The GPW dataset began as a collaboration between CIESIN and the National Center for Geographic Information and Analysis (NCGIA). It provided the first detailed population density distribution for the world using Geographic Information System (GIS) methods. Such a gridded product facilitates integration of population data with other types of environmental data collected on a regular grid, e.g., remotely sensed data from satellites. Version 2 of GPW (http://sedac.ciesin.columbia.edu/plue/gpw), developed jointly with the International Food Policy Research Institute and the World Resources Institute, reflects an accumulating database and associated body of knowledge about subnational administrative boundaries for the world's countries and their populations. GPW has been cited widely in the peer-reviewed scientific literature, and more generally in many policy- and education-oriented documents, including such publications as *Nature*, *Scientific American*, the *Quarterly Journal of Economics*, the *World Resources* reports, and *The New York Times*.

Environmental Treaties and Resource Indicators (ENTRI)

The ENTRI database provides interactive access to an online database of international environmental treaties, treaty summaries, and various national-level environmental, natural resource, and socioeconomic indicators (http://sedac.ciesin.columbia.edu/entri). Data were obtained from a variety of academic, governmental, and nongovernmental sources. ENTRI is widely used in the international relations community and by those involved in education on international environmental policy. Enhancements currently in progress include the addition of a large number of new treaty texts, addition of new indexing and search capabilities, and updating of the query interface.

Environmental Sustainability Indicators (ESI)

The ESI represents a collaboration between CIESIN and the Yale Center for Environmental Law and Policy and the Global Leaders for Tomorrow Environment Task Force of the World Economic Forum. It is designed to meet the needs of policy analysts and decision-makers concerned about progress towards environmental sustainability—in an arena where there is little consensus on what constitutes true environmental sustainability. Drawing on both a broad theoretical framework and practical experience in working with national-level environmental and socioeconomic data, CIESIN developed a flexible, multi-dimensional framework for assessing relative progress towards sustainability. By making the detailed data available (http://www.ciesin.columbia.edu/indicators/ESI/), CIESIN permits others to work with the data, including use of different "weighting" schemes to reflect different normative perspectives. An online mapping tool (http://maps.ciesin.columbia.edu/esi) also permits users to visualize and compare the ESI with other major national-level indicators such as the Human Development Index.

Intergovernmental Panel on Climate Change (IPCC) Special Report on Emission Scenarios

In collaboration with IPCC Working Group 3, CIESIN supported an "open process" to permit greater input from around the world during the development of the IPCC *Special Report on Emission Scenarios* (Nakicenovic and Swart, 2000). After the alternative scenarios of future global greenhouse gas emissions had been completed and reviewed, CIESIN archived and began disseminating the scenarios to permit a range of climate modelers and other global change researchers to use the scenarios in further assessments of the implications of future emissions. CIESIN also began collecting and archiving the inputs and outputs of key computer models used to generate SRES scenarios. Although these data are not based on "observations" per se, they do represent a unique source of information about the state of knowledge of human-environment systems as embodied in computer simulation models. CIESIN is currently working with the IPCC Task Group on Scenarios for Climate Impact Assessment to improve the usability and accessibility of SRES data for impact assessment studies to be carried out prior to the 4th IPCC assessment.

Population Environment Research Network

In an effort to reach a specific subgroup of the global change research community, CIESIN has partnered with the International Union for the Scientific Study of Population (IUSSP), the International Human Dimensions Programme on Global Environmental Change (IHDP), and the John D. and Catherine T. MacArthur Foundation in establishing the Population Environment Research Network (http://www.populationenvironmentresearch.org). CIESIN hosts the network's Web site and discussion lists, and helps to maintain its online resources including a database of research on population-environment interactions. CIESIN staff participate actively in the regular "cyberseminars" organized by the network and contribute to other network activities and resources.

FUTURE DIRECTIONS

Rapid changes in data collection methods, information and communications technology, and user expectations during the past decade underscore the need for data centers to respond flexibly and proactively to changing scientific and user needs. Stagnant or declining budgets also place severe pressures on data centers to find ways to do more with fewer resources. At the same time, data centers have important responsibilities related to long-term data stewardship, including preservation of critical data, associated documentation, and data accessibility.

By relocating to a major research university, and in particular, by joining an innovative, interdisciplinary initiative, the Earth Institute at Columbia University, CIESIN has attempted to position itself to take advantage of a wider range of collaborative partnerships not only within the University, but also across the New York metropolitan region, the U.S., and the world. Ongoing partnerships include:

- development of a global "wild areas" database in collaboration with the Wildlife Conservation Society and the Center for Environmental Research and Conservation;
- participation in a major international, interdisciplinary research project on arsenic and lead contamination in Bangladesh and the U.S. with the Columbia School of Public Health and other units;
- collaboration with the Open GIS Consortium and with several New York City agencies and organizations on the development of interoperable Web-mapping systems; and
- collaboration with the Global Change Information and Research Center of the Chinese Academy of Sciences to promote access to data on China.

It is also essential for existing data centers to collaborate more proactively to share technologies and processes, promote interdisciplinary data management, and address pressing data policy issues. CIESIN has recently led the development of a strategic plan for the ICSU World Data Center system, which encompasses more than 45 data centers around the world, and is also an active member of the so-called DAAC Alliance, a confederation of the 8 NASA-supported Distributed Active Archive Centers and the Global Hydrology Resource Center. A number of CIESIN staff are involved in data management and data policy activities sponsored by the U.S. National Research Council and by ICSU's CODATA, and in various activities of the NASA Federation of Earth Science Information Partners.

Currently, CIESIN is reviewing its data management, digital archiving, and records management practices to improve the processes supporting development and maintenance of its products and services and to seek ways to facilitate greater integration across projects and processes. It is expected that revising these practices and the supporting systems will facilitate greater efficiency within the data center by enabling knowledge management, improving workflow, and increasing communication among project participants. CIESIN is also monitoring the potential implications of new Office of Management and Budget regulations concerning data quality, which may have a significant impact on Federal data management and dissemination activities.

Improvements in digital archiving would facilitate digital preservation within an evolving technological infrastructure. CIESIN has begun to explore the Open Archival Information System (OAIS) model for digital archiving to facilitate long-term digital preservation and continual access and use despite changes in information and communication technology. The OAIS model recommends the creation of archival information packages to facilitate recovery and preserve digital resources for long-term access and use (CCSDS, 1999). The requirements for data management and digital archiving are being reviewed to identify specifications for the database design and the new procedures that would be implemented to meet the objectives of both initiatives.

An increasing focus on data interoperability is an essential element of this approach. CIESIN's current efforts with the Open GIS Consortium suggest new ways to support and maintain interoperable access to spatial data, which constitute a significant portion of CIESIN's data holdings. However, other aspects of data and metadata interoperability also need to be explored, e.g., relative to socioeconomic data formats, model-generated data, and interoperable data services.

CONCLUSION

CIESIN serves the GEC research community by cooperatively working with community members to identify their needs and explore opportunities for supporting their research efforts. Collaborative activities engaging interdisciplinary staff and community groups have contributed to existing data management and support operations and to designing and developing new products and services to foster research on the environment. The staff of CIESIN will continue to explore ways to engage the GEC research community in participatory design, decision-making, and cooperative development activities to improve its processes and the resulting products and services offered to meet the needs of users around the world.

REFERENCES

Consultative Committee for Space Data Systems. 1999. CCSDS 650.0-R-1: *Reference Model for an Open Archival Information System: Draft Recommendation for Space Data System Standards*. Red Book. Issue 1, May 1999. Accessed 7 April 2002 from: http://www.ccsds.org/documents/pdf/CCSDS-650.0-R-1.pdf.

Chen, R.S. 1981. Interdisciplinary research and integration: The case of CO_2 and climate. *Climatic Change* 3: 429-47. Also published in Chen, R.S., E. Boulding, and S. Schneider (Eds.), *Social Science Research and Climate Change: An Interdisciplinary Appraisal*. D. Reidel Publishing Co. 1983: 230-248.

Downs, R. R. 2001. Managing End-User Development of Digital Library Resources to Support User Communities. In M. E. Williams (Ed.), *Proceedings of the 22nd National Online Meeting*, May 15-17, 2001, New York, NY: 133-138.

Hurd, J. M. 2000. The Transformation of Scientific Communication. *Journal of the American Society for Information Science*, 51(14): 1279-1283.

Kates, R. W., W. C. Clark, R. Corell, J. M. Hall, C. C. Jaeger, I. Lowe, J. J. McCarthy, H.J. Schellnhuber, B. Bolin, N. M. Dickson, Sylvie Faucheux, Gilberto C. Gallopin, Arnulf Gruebler, Brian Huntley, J. Jäger, N. S. Jodha, R. E. Kasperson, A. Mabogunje, P. Matson, H. Mooney, B. Moore III, T. O'Riordan, and U. Svedin. 2001. Sustainability science. *Science* 292, no. 5517 (27 April 2001): 641-642.

McCain, K. W. 2000. Sharing Digitized Research-Related Information on the World Wide Web. *Journal of the American Society for Information Science*, 51(14): 1321-1327.

McGlamery, P. 1999. Magic: A Connecticut Collection of Geodata for the Geo-Scientist. *Science & Technology Libraries*, 17(3/4), 209-216. Printed simultaneously in D. Stern (Ed.), *Digital Libraries: Philosophies, Technical Design Considerations, and Example Scenarios*. The Haworth Press, Inc. 1999: 209-216.

Nakicenovic, N. and Swart, R., eds. 2000. *Special Report on Emissions Scenarios*. Cambridge University Press, Cambridge, United Kingdom, 612 pp.

National Research Council. 2000. *The Science of Regional and Global Change: Putting Knowledge to Work*. Washington DC: National Academy Press. 32 pp.

Beyond Bibliography:
A Dynamic Approach to the Cataloging
of Multidisciplinary Environmental Data
for Global Change Research

Gene R. Major

SUMMARY. Global environmental change is a complex issue requiring observations and data from many different Earth science disciplines. The Earth science community has made a vast amount of data and information widely available on the Internet for global change research. However, while there are many tools for locating global change literature, there are relatively few tools to aid librarians, researchers and others in locating global change data. The NASA Global Change Master Directory (GCMD) (http://gcmd.nasa.gov) is a dynamic multidisciplinary information retrieval system consisting of metadata records that describe Earth science data sets, where data are located, and how to obtain the data. This article describes the role of the GCMD in locating and accessing global change data, the structure of

Gene R. Major, BS (Math/Physics), MS (Physics), MS (Library and Information Studies), is GCMD lead Earth Science Coordinator and GCMD task leader at Science Systems and Applications, Inc., Lanham, MD (E-mail: major@gcmd.nasa.gov).

The author gratefully acknowledges the support of the NASA GCMD Project Manager, Lola M. Olsen (E-mail: olsen@gcmd.nasa.gov), NASA/GSFC, Greenbelt, MD 20771.

This work was performed under NASA contract #NAS5-00220.

[Haworth co-indexing entry note]: "Beyond Bibliography: A Dynamic Approach to the Cataloging of Multidisciplinary Environmental Data for Global Change Research." Major, Gene R. Co-published simultaneously in *Science & Technology Libraries* (The Haworth Information Press, an imprint of The Haworth Press, Inc.) Vol. 23, No. 4, 2003, pp. 21-36; and: *Online Ecological and Environmental Data* (ed: Virginia Baldwin) The Haworth Information Press, an imprint of The Haworth Press, Inc., 2003, pp. 21-36. Single or multiple copies of this article are available for a fee from The Haworth Document Delivery Service [1-800-HAWORTH, 9:00 a.m. - 5:00 p.m. (EST). E-mail address: docdelivery@haworthpress.com].

Digital Object Identifier: 10.1300/J122v23n04_03

metadata describing the data, the development of controlled vocabularies to search for data, and the implementation of interfaces for the retrieval of global change data set information. The GCMD, as a catalog of global change data, provides librarians and researchers a tool to meet the global change data and information needs of the user community. *[Article copies available for a fee from The Haworth Document Delivery Service: 1-800-HAWORTH. E-mail address: <docdelivery@haworthpress.com> Website: <http://www.HaworthPress.com> © 2003 by The Haworth Press, Inc. All rights reserved.]*

KEYWORDS. Global change, environmental information, databases, information retrieval systems, controlled vocabularies, metadata, keywords, search and retrieval, Earth science data

INTRODUCTION

Global environmental change is one of the most important scientific issues of our times. Understanding global environmental change requires a multidisciplinary approach to research–unparalleled in other scientific endeavors. Oceanographers require data collected by atmospheric scientists to study the El Nino/La Nina phenomena; climatologists need access to geologic data to model past climate conditions; ecologists need access to remotely-sensed data from Earth-orbiting satellites. Even health researchers require climate and ecological data to understand the vectors of insect- and human-borne diseases due to environmental and climate changes. An intergovernmental panel of distinguished scientists has concluded that "there is new and stronger evidence that most of the warming observed over the past 50 years is attributable to human activities" (Houghton et al., 2001). A panel of scientists commissioned by the National Academy of Scientists (NAS, 2001) corroborated the findings of the Intergovernmental Panel on Climate Change (IPCC).

Many U.S. Federal agencies as well as international organizations are undertaking global change research to provide data and information to make informed policy decisions. The cornerstone of informed decision-making is the availability and access to global environmental change data and information. The National Research Council (1998) stated that "[u]ltimately, the [U.S. Global Change Research Program] USGCRP is about information . . . the subject of the program's research demands that information flow effectively to the public at large as well as to researchers." The impact and role of the libraries to impart knowledge through dissemination of information about global change to the public and researchers cannot be underestimated (Rand, 1995).

As part of the scientific communication process, global change research results are disseminated through technical reports, conferences, and peer-reviewed literature. The traditional print-based system that relies on the refereed scientific journal as the key delivery mechanism for research findings is undergoing a transformation to a system much more reliant on electronic communication and storage media (Hurd, 2000). With electronic technologies commonplace, the availability and sharing of data have also become an integral part of the modern scientific communication process. The Earth science community, in particular, has made a vast amount of data and information widely available on the Internet; however, there are relatively few tools to aid librarians and researchers in locating these data.

NASA's GLOBAL CHANGE MASTER DIRECTORY

Scope of the GCMD Collection of Earth Science Data Set Descriptions

NASA's Global Change Master Directory (GCMD) (http://gcmd.nasa.gov) is analogous to a traditional bibliographic information retrieval system; however, instead of containing records that provide access to literature, the GCMD holds records that describe Earth science data sets relevant to environmental and global change research (Figure 1). The GCMD information retrieval system holds over 13,500 records–modest by the size of many library catalogs, but representative of a significant amount of Earth science data for global change research published by, and available to, the research community.

The GCMD, as an information retrieval system, satisfies the core elements of traditional bibliographic databases familiar to librarians:

- a database to store records
- a record that defines the logical format of the information
- a query capability that allows users or systems to conduct searches
- a results set or list of titles from the database that meet search criteria
- retrieved results from the database presented in a form readable by the user or in a format that can be interpreted by another networked computer system

The scope of the GCMD database covers nearly every aspect of global change research:

- Agriculture and food production
- Atmosphere, meteorology and climatology
- Biosphere, biodiversity, and ecosystems studies
- Oceanography and ocean-atmosphere climate systems such al El Nino
- Land surface processes and land cover changes
- Snow and ice dynamics including glaciological and polar processes

- Human dimensions of climate change such as land use, population and health
- Hydrology, including surface and ground water processes
- Past climate changes, including ice core and tree ring studies (paleoclimatology)
- Sun-earth connections
- Geophysics and geological processes

Records from atmospheric science disciplines account for 18% of the GCMD holdings, followed closely by biosphere studies at 17% and ocean science and land surface processes at 13%.

The GCMD database entries describe data taken from all geographic areas of the world and all time periods. Data sets can be global in nature, such as those derived from Earth-orbiting satellites, or focused on a single point on the globe, such as an ecosystem study. All ranges of time periods are covered as

FIGURE 1. NASA Global Change Master Directory (GCMD) Home Page

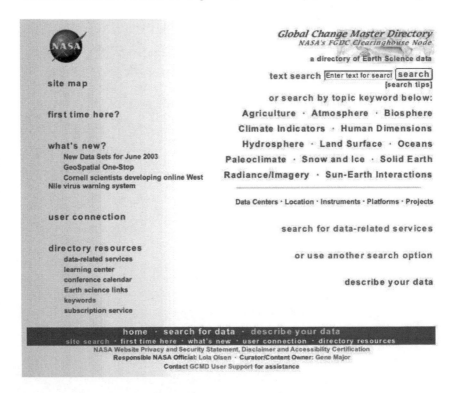

well, including geologic and historical periods that extend thousands of years into the past, to ongoing scientific projects collecting data today.

The body of data for global change research is collected from a wide variety of instrumentation. About 42% of the GCMD database entries describe data collected by space-borne sensors. More than half of the GCMD database represents data collected from *in-situ* instruments such as on-board ships, aircraft, and from ground-based observing stations.

Nearly every country is represented as a data provider. Investigators are located in universities and agencies throughout the world, and many contribute data to national and international archives. In the United States, data are available from NASA, the National Oceanic and Atmospheric Administration (NOAA), the Department of Energy (DOE), the U.S. Geological Survey (USGS), the Environmental Protection Agency (EPA), and the U.S. Department of Agriculture (USDA), as well as from universities and scientific institutions. The GCMD collaborates with a number of international projects such as the Committee on Earth Observation Satellites (CEOS), the International Geosphere-Biosphere Programme (IGBP), the United Nations, the Joint Committee on Antarctic Data Management (JCADM), and the World Data Centers (WDCs). Data set descriptions derived from these projects, as well as from individual researchers and smaller projects, are also represented.

Metadata and the Organization of Earth Science Information in the GCMD

Metadata has become a buzzword for descriptions about digital resources. Metadata, of course, has been integral to the library community since the time libraries have been in existence. A metadata record is a surrogate for the original work and, as a concept, is really not that different from traditional bibliographic document representation. The geospatial community has been involved in the standardization of metadata relevant to Geographic Information Systems (GIS) (Guptil, 1999). However, metadata, as conceptualized by the geospatial data community, was mainly applied as *use* metadata–how to use the data, the format of the data, organization of files, etc. Little attention was paid to *semantic* metadata–information that will assist the user in the discovery of data through the use of controlled vocabularies and well-structured text. The current development of content standards, such as Federal Geographic Data Committee (FGDC) Content Standard for Digital Geospatial Metadata (http://www.fgdc. gov/metadata/contstan.html) and the International Standards Organization Metadata Standard for Geographic Information/Geomatics, ISO 19115/TC 211 (http://www.isotc211.org/) for geospatial data are more concerned with establishing metadata fields rather than what content is actually contained in those fields (Milstead and Feldman, 1999).

At the core of the GCMD are well-structured metadata records designed for semantic search and retrieval and interoperability across multiple computer systems. The GCMD metadata follows the Directory Interchange Format (DIF) metadata format (http://gcmd.nasa.gov/User/difguide/difman.html), which was developed specifically with the end-user in mind for the search and retrieval of Earth science data. Central to that goal was the development of controlled vocabularies to index the metadata records and the development of software that checks the validity of those vocabularies when new metadata records are processed (Pollack et al., 2001). Controlled vocabularies have been developed for:

- Earth science parameter keywords
- Source (or platform) keywords
- Sensor (or instrumentation) keywords
- Geographic location keywords
- Project or field campaign keywords
- Data center names

To further enhance the search and retrieval of information, text fields are included such as a summary, title, references, use and access constraints, quality of the data, and non-controlled keywords. Additional fields describe data providers, data distribution information, and data set citation details. The GCMD provides direct access to the Earth science data set being described (where possible). Particularly valuable to the researcher is the ability to hyperlink directly from the metadata record to the actual data set that can then be downloaded or manipulated through another interface. The availability of such a system is an important component of a new paradigm of Earth science scientific communication.

Controlled Vocabularies for Describing Earth Science Data Sets

Successful retrieval of documents depends on well-structured metadata and comprehensive indexing of records with keywords from the controlled vocabulary, combined with well-populated text fields to enhance free-text searching. An extensive Earth science parameter keyword vocabulary has been developed to describe Earth science data products that could be used for global change research.

Earth science parameter keywords are arranged in a 3-tiered hierarchy with an optional uncontrolled keyword as part of the hierarchy to provide more detailed descriptors. Every entry in the GCMD is indexed with one or more of these hierarchical science parameter keywords. Controlled keywords are added to the database based on data provider needs and adherence to rules and procedures (which are readily available online). The syntax of the science parameter keyword hierarchy is:

TOPIC>TERM>VARIABLE>detailed variable

where TOPIC, TERM, and VARIABLE are controlled and the *detailed variable* is an uncontrolled, yet searchable word or phrase that provides a higher level of descriptor detail.

In the example:

Oceans > Ocean Chemistry > Carbon Dioxide > partial carbon dioxide

Oceans is the TOPIC.
Ocean Chemistry is the TERM.
Carbon Dioxide is the VARIABLE.
partial carbon dioxide is a free text, uncontrolled detailed variable.

GCMD Earth science subject descriptors consist of 13 TOPICs corresponding to the research areas described above. These high-level TOPICs, are used to define subject areas describing global change data:

- *Agriculture*–for data related to agriculture, food resources, and natural resources
- *Atmosphere*–for meteorological, atmospheric and climate data
- *Biosphere*–for ecosystem and biodiversity data
- *Climate Indicators*–for important climate indices such as drought indices and atmospheric circulation patterns
- *Cryosphere*–for snow, ice, glaciological and polar data
- *Hydrosphere*–for surface and groundwater data
- *Land Surface*–for data related to land use, land cover, and land resources
- *Human Dimensions*–for data related to the human dimensions of climate change such as human health, population, and environmental impacts
- *Oceans*–for marine and oceanographic data, ocean-atmosphere climatology and marine biology data
- *Paleoclimatology*–for data related to the study of Earth's past climate including data collected from ice cores and tree rings
- *Solid Earth*–for data related to geophysics and solid Earth such as plate tectonics, volcanism, and geological processes

- *Solar-Terrestrial Interactions*–for data related to Sun-Earth geophysical interactions and solar irradiance affects on climate
- *Radiance and Imagery*–for imagery and instrument-level data directly derived from satellite and aircraft imaging sensors (such as Landsat imagery)

Over 1,050 TERMs and VARIABLEs complete the science keyword hierarchy. An example of a partial set of TERMs and VARIABLEs for the TOPIC *Land Surface* is shown below (for a complete list see: http://gcmd.nasa.gov/Resources/valids/gcmd_parameters.html).

```
Land Surface > Land Use/Land Cover > Land Cover
Land Surface > Land Use/Land Cover > Land Productivity
Land Surface > Land Use/Land Cover > Land Resources
Land Surface > Land Use/Land Cover > Land Use Classes

Land Surface > Surface Radiative Properties > Albedo
Land Surface > Surface Radiative Properties > Anisotropy
Land Surface > Surface Radiative Properties > Emissivity
Land Surface > Surface Radiative Properties > Reflectance
Land Surface > Surface Radiative Properties > Thermal Properties
```

Other controlled vocabularies include:

- *Geographic locations* topically organized by continent region, body of water, country, and geophysical location. [Note: the GCMD is planning on altering the geographic keyword structure.] For example:

  Body of Water > Pacific Ocean
  will become
  Oceans > Pacific

- *Source or platform* organized by type of platform: aircraft, balloons/rockets, *in situ* land-based sources, *in situ* ocean-based sources, interplanetary spacecraft, maps/charts/models, satellites, space stations/manned spacecraft. For example:

  Satellites > EOS TERRA

- *Sensor or instrument* organized by type of sensor: altimeters, cameras, *in situ* sensors, laboratory sensors, lidars/lasers, magnetic sensors, photometers, positioning/navigation devices, radars, scatterometers, seismic sensors, sonar/acoustic sensors, sounders/profilers, spectral/radiation sensors, telescopes. For example:

  Spectral/Radiation Sensors > MODIS > MODerate-Resolution Imaging Spectroradiometer

- *Project or field campaign* organized alphabetically. For example:

ARM > Atmospheric Radiation Measurement Program

The distribution of controlled Earth science parameters among the records within the GCMD database closely follows patterns typical of the statistical properties of bibliographic full-text databases (Bates, 1998). While a few terms are used to populate many records, the majority of terms populate few records.

SEARCH AND RETRIEVAL:
LOCATING EARTH SCIENCE DATASETS

The GCMD is a Web-based search and retrieval system. Users can search the GCMD using controlled vocabularies or using free-text or a combination of both. Controlled vocabulary and free-text searches are two independent, but complementary information retrieval systems within GCMD.

Search and Retrieval by Controlled Vocabulary

Searches conducted using the controlled vocabulary match the chosen word in the metadata record using a direct search of the database. Users can select from among any of the twelve science keyword TOPICs (subject areas) discussed previously, and then select from the terms and variables that would be most appropriate for their search. Results can be refined by adding another science parameter, by combining with other controlled keywords, or by adding a free-text component to the search (Figure 2).

After a keyword selection is made and the query is submitted, a results set of Earth science data set titles is returned. Selecting a title will retrieve the metadata record in a "brief record" format with the option of selecting the "full record" or navigating to other sections of the displayed metadata record (Figure 3). Keywords within the displayed record are hyperlinked, so the user can perform searches of the database directly from the displayed record.

Search and Retrieval by Free-Text

Free-text search and retrieval uses a customized implementation of the ANSI/NISO Z39.50 protocol with ranked results based on a vector model. Searches by free-text can be made by entering single or multiple words (for phrase searching) and simple Boolean AND/OR for words or phrases occurring anywhere in the text.

Other search features:

Geospatial Search–users can query on a specific geographic location or enter their own geographic coordinates. Geographic locations can be selected from the controlled list. Geospatial coordinates can be specified or "drawn" on a Java map applet to assist users who are unsure of the geographic coordinates for their area of interest.

Temporal Search–users can restrict their search to a date or a range of dates.

Fielded Search–users can also restrict their search to specific fields within the metadata record to increase precision. For example, users can restrict their free-text search to the title field only if desired. Free-text searches can also be combined with controlled vocabulary searches to increase precision.

Adding Records to the GCMD

Online Web-based tools (http://gcmd.nasa.gov/cgi-bin/difbuilder/difbuilder) have been developed to add metadata records to the GCMD database. Although the metadata follows the Directory Interchange Format (DIF) (http://gcmd.nasa. gov/User/difguide/difman.html), the data provider or metadata author, as cataloger of the data, does not need to know metadata syntax when using the online

FIGURE 2. NASA Global Change Master Directory (GCMD)–Atmosphere

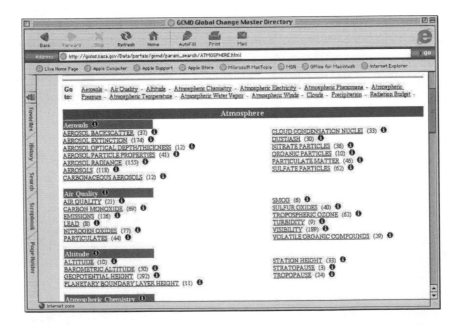

FIGURE 3. NASA Global Change Master Directory (GCMD) Search Results

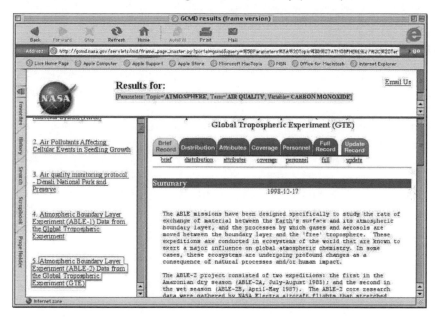

tools. Only six fields are minimally required for completion of a data set description, although up to 33 fields can be completed. Of course, the more complete the record, the better the chances are for the record to be retrieved during a search. Upon completion, the data provider can automatically submit the record by e-mail to the GCMD staff where quality control procedures are performed. After the record is entered into the database, the record can be searched and retrieved. Metadata authors and data providers can update their metadata records directly from the displayed record (Figure 4).

DYNAMIC APPROACH TO DATA SET CATALOGING: ACCESS TO DATA

The GCMD is not a static catalog. The retrieval of data set descriptions is but one aspect of a dynamic, interoperable system that takes full advantage of Web-based technologies to assist users in locating and accessing data. The GCMD is engaged in the following functional areas to provide access to data from meta-data records:

- Direct access to data for research and educational purposes.
- Citation information for data sets.
- Shared metadata entries using object-oriented technologies.

Direct Access to Data

Perhaps the greatest value of the retrieved record from the GCMD is the functionality to link directly to a data set. Of course, not all data sets are available online, but many are. Direct access to the data is from the DIF metadata field, "Related_URL". This provides the user an exceptional tool–not only for discovering and locating the data, but also for obtaining the data itself. In the publishing and bibliographic control industry, analogous developments exist in linking the surrogate or bibliographic metadata record to the object itself (a journal article or e-publication) (Caplan and Arms, 1999).

As an example, the Related_URL group below identifies the type of URL being linked, the URL (hyperlinked), and a short description of the resource. In this case, the URL takes the user directly to the data set and additional on-line documentation.

FIGURE 4. Life Cycle of the Directory Interchange Format (DIF)

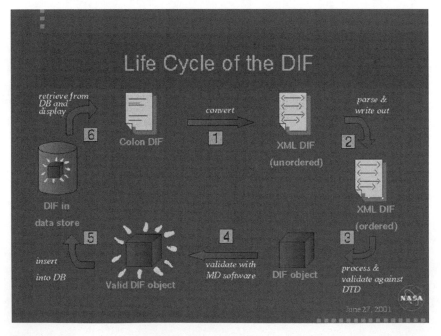

Group: Related_URL

> **Content Type:** ASSOCIATED DATA SET(S)
> **URL:** http://cdiac.esd.ornl.gov/ftp/ndp001/
> **Description:** Access to Mauna Loa carbon dioxide NDP-001 data

End_Group

Citation Information for Data Sets

The citation of a data set is as important to the data provider as the citation of a journal article. The DIF metadata field, "Data_Set_Citation", provides fields for how a data set should be cited in the scientific literature and for proper acknowledgement and credit to the data producer. The Data Set Citation field consists of the following elements:

```
Group: Data_Set_Citation
        Dataset_Creator:
        Dataset_Title:
        Dataset_Series_Name:
            Dataset_Release_Date:
            Dataset_Release_Place:
            Dataset_Publisher:
            Version:
            Issue_Identification:
            Data_Presentation_Form:
            Other_Citation_Details:
            Online Resource:
    End_Group
```

Where,

Dataset_Creator is the name of the organization(s) or individual(s) with primary intellectual responsibility for the data set's development.

Dataset_Title is the title of the data set.

Dataset_Series_Name is the name of the dataset series, or aggregate dataset of which the dataset is a part.

Issue_Identification is the volume or issue number of the publication (if applicable).

Dataset_Release_Date is the date when the data set was made available for release.

Dataset_Release_Place is the name of the city (and state or province and country, if needed) where the data set was made available for release.

Dataset_Publisher is the name of the individual or organization that made the data set available for release.

Version is the version of the data set.

Data_Presentation_Form is the mode in which the data are represented, e.g., atlas, image, profile, etc.

Other_Citation_Details allows for additional citation information.

Online Resource is the URL of the data set.

Shared Metadata Records

Libraries have a catalog record-sharing mechanism through the Online Computer Library Center (OCLC) or the Research Libraries Information Network (RLIN) for bibliographic (and now Internet) records using MARC (or Dublin Core). Yet metadata describing data sets are often found in varying formats, on different platforms, and using different storage systems making interoperability difficult or impossible. Global change research depends on access to multi-disciplinary Earth science data and metadata, which tend to reside in heterogeneous, distributed systems. Recent advances in object-oriented architectures using eXtensible Markup Language (XML) technologies are providing exciting frameworks for sharing data and metadata across multiple, disparate systems. The GCMD is using these technologies to increase interoperability among metadata systems.

Metadata records are represented internally in the GCMD as XML documents. A Document Type Definition (DTD) structure has been developed, allowing the use of tools such as XML parsers and stylesheet processors, along with Java-based technologies to create an environment of shared metadata regardless of format or platform. Participating organizations can send XML metadata documents, which can then be broadcast to other participating organizations using Java's Remote Method Invocation (RMI) object broker (Kendig et al., 2000). Syntactic and semantic validation of metadata documents are controlled by the GCMD–an initial version of authority control for data set descriptions that allows for distributed sharing of metadata documents among systems and a comprehensive, external view to the user.

Data Availability and the Scientific Communication Process

Modern scientific communication is at a crossroads (Lucky, 2000). Never before have such a vast amount of data and information been available at near instantaneous speeds using the Internet and the Web. The process of disseminating scientific information formerly took months to years but can now be done nearly instantaneously using the Internet, e-mail, listservs, e-conferences, e-publications, and other Web technologies. Earth science data–some in near-realtime–can now be made routinely available and accessible using ftp and the Web for easy down-loading.

However, unlike print publications, data can be ephemeral–held in the hands of the scientist until the research paper is written and published, only to vanish. Data for global change research requires more longevity and permanence. Electronic technologies have helped in the storage and availability of data through Web-based and ftp servers, but there is little commonality among data and metadata types and among Earth science disciplines. Advances in new Web technologies have made it possible to integrate and interoperate with distributed metadata systems, such as the GCMD, so that metadata and information can be shared across networks and multiple metadata systems. Improvements in XML and Java technologies will enhance the user experience and provide researchers with greater access to global change data through the GCMD.

Global environmental change is an issue that demands the attention of not only the research scientist, but also the general public. The value of global research can be realized through greater accessibility to data and information to make informed decisions about the global environment. Librarians have always played a crucial role in making information accessible to further knowledge. The GCMD as a data catalog and access system provides librarians and researchers with a tool to meet the global change data and information needs of the user community to advance our understanding of the global environment.

REFERENCES

Bates, M.J. 1998. "Indexing and access for digital libraries and the Internet: Human, database, and domain factors." *Journal of the American Society for Information Science*, 49 (13): 1185-1205.

Caplan, P. and W. Y. Arms. 1999. "Reference Linking for Journal Articles." *D-Lib Magazine*, 5 (78). http://www.dlib.org/dlib/july99/caplan/07caplan.html.

Guptil, S. C. 1999. "Metadata and Data Catalogues." In Longley, P.A., M.F. Goodchild, D.J. Maguire, and D.W. Rhind, eds. *Geographical Information Systems*, Vol. 2, 2nd ed., NY: John Wiley & Sons.

Houghton, J.T., Y. Ding, D.J. Griggs, M. Noguer, P. J. van der Linden and D. Xiaosu, eds. 2001. Climate Change 2001: The Scientific Basis–Contribution of Working Group I to the Third Assessment Report of the Intergovernmental Panel on Climate Change (IPCC). Cambridge: Cambridge University Press, 994 pp.

Hurd, J. M. 2000. "The transformation of scientific communication: A model for 2020," *Journal of the American Society for Information Science*, 51 (14): 1279-1283.

Kendig, D., C. Gokey, R.T. Northcutt, L. Olsen, O. Bukhres, S. Sikkupparbathyam. 2000. "Metadata sharing among distributed heterogeneous databases using Java technology: A turn-key solution." Presented at the EO/GEO 17-19, April 2000, London, England. http://gcmd.gsfc.nasa.gov/Aboutus/presentations/conferences/EOGEO2000/MD8/EOGEO_Abstract.html.

Lucky, R. 2000. "The Quickening of Science Communication." *Science*, 289: 259-269.

Milstead, J. and S. Feldman. 1999. "Metadata: Cataloging by any Other Name." Online http://www.onlinemag.net/OL1999/milstead1.html.

National Academy of Sciences. 2001. "Climate Change Science: An analysis of some key questions." Committee on the Science of Climate Change, Division on Earth and Life Studies, National Research Council, Washington, DC: National Academy Press.

National Research Council (NRC). 1998. "Global environmental change: Research pathways for the next decade." National Research Council Committee on Global Change Research, Board on Sustainable Development Policy, Policy Division, Washington, DC: National Academy Press.

Pollack, J., C. Gokey, D. Kendig, and L. Olsen. 2001. "Syntactic and semantic validation within a metadata management system." Presented at the EO/GEO July 2001, Fredericton, New Brunswick, Canada. http://gcmd.gsfc.nasa.gov/Aboutus/presentations/conferences/eogeo01/eogeo_01.html.

Rand, R.Y., (ed.), 1995. "Global change research and the role of libraries," *Library Hi Tech*, 13, (1-2): 7-86.

A National Environmental Data Network Revealed Through the Study of Acid Rain

Frederick W. Stoss

SUMMARY. The topic generally known as acid rain presents a series of data and information challenges to researchers, policy makers, educators, and librarians and information specialists. Acid rain became one of the first and, at the time, one of the largest and most vexing environmental problems of a global scale in terms of both its origins and its solutions. The transport of air pollutants over long distances had been postulated as early as the 17th century. Scientific study of the chemical composition of the Earth's atmosphere began in earnest in the later half of the 19th century and continues today. This paper examines the development of a national network of environmental data-gathering activities revealed from decades of acid rain research in the United States, ranging from nationally coordinated, interagency research programs to state sponsored ecosystem and sub-ecosystem studies and data monitoring activities. *[Article copies available for a fee from The Haworth Document Delivery Service: 1-800-HAWORTH. E-mail address: <docdelivery@haworthpress.com> Website: <http://www.HaworthPress.com> © 2003 by The Haworth Press, Inc. All rights reserved.]*

KEYWORDS. Acid precipitation, acid rain, data archives, databases, ecology, ecological data, ecological information, Long-Term Ecological Re-

Frederick W. Stoss, MS (Zoology/Ecology), MLS, is Associate Librarian, Science and Engineering Library, State University of New York at Buffalo, Buffalo, NY 14260 (E-mail: fstoss@buffalo.edu).

[Haworth co-indexing entry note]: "A National Environmental Data Network Revealed Through the Study of Acid Rain." Stoss, Frederick W. Co-published simultaneously in *Science & Technology Libraries* (The Haworth Information Press, an imprint of The Haworth Press, Inc.) Vol. 23, No. 4, 2003, pp. 37-57; and: *Online Ecological and Environmental Data* (ed: Virginia Baldwin) The Haworth Information Press, an imprint of The Haworth Press, Inc., 2003, pp. 37-57. Single or multiple copies of this article are available for a fee from The Haworth Document Delivery Service [1-800-HAWORTH, 9:00 a.m. - 5:00 p.m. (EST). E-mail address: docdelivery@haworthpress.com].

http://www.haworthpress.com/web/STL
© 2003 by The Haworth Press, Inc. All rights reserved.
Digital Object Identifier: 10.1300/J122v23n04_04

search Network, Man and the Biosphere Program, National Atmospheric Deposition Program

INTRODUCTION

Like many of today's environmental problems the causes and sources of acid rain (or acidic precipitation or acidic deposition) have no respect for political boundaries. The polluting sources of acid rain may be found hundreds or thousands of miles up-wind from the ecosystems suffering adverse effects. The long-range transport of pollution in the Earth's atmosphere requires inter-regional and international cooperation and exchanges of research data and technologies to identify the causes, effects, remediation, and reduction or, hopefully, the elimination of the causes of acid rain.

In addition to the exchange of scientific and technical research data is the need to broadly disseminate the resulting data and information bases among all parties involved in the study of the problem of acid rain: the interdisciplinary communities of researchers, policy makers, managers, administrators, educators, and students. This dissemination of data and information across disciplines and lines of work is necessary to stimulate and sustain the exchanges across disciplines for the ideas and proposals to reduce the causes and effects of acid rain.

There are four major data and information challenges revealed as a result of multidisciplinary studies related to acid rain: the growth of the data and information base reporting the results of research on the topic; the rapid growth and dispersion of the information base among the multidisciplinary communities generating and consuming this data and information base; the rapid changes in information technologies required to identify, acquire, archive, disseminate, and utilize the data and information resulting from research and policy analyses; and the need to assure equity in the access to this data and information across disciplines, lines of work, corporate or individual lines of thought or need.

ACID RAIN RESEARCH IN A HISTORICAL PERSPECTIVE BUILDS A DATA BASE

Scientific and technical information is derived from data and recording the results of research from laboratory and fields studies, monitoring campaigns, modeling strategies, and other activities. The topic of acid rain has a rather long information trail and a rich history revealed in its literature.

Ellis Cowling[1] provided the first major historical review of the acid rain problem and traced the relationships between human activities and their impact to the environment. Cowling cites studies by Evelyn in 1661 and Graunt in 1662 who noted the influences of industrial air emissions to plants and humans and the transboundary transport of air pollutants between England and France. Cowling attributes the first use of the term "acid rain" to R. A. Smith in an 1872 book *Air and Rain: The Beginnings of a Chemical Climatology* (London, Longmans, Green), who noted chemical variations in the chemistry of rain water and the influence of the combustion of coal, direction of the wind, and proximity to the sea as affecting the damage to plant life and materials exposed to rain water.

The early decades of the 20th century saw a small number of scientific articles continuing to monitor the acid content of rain in Australia,[2] the United States,[3] Uithuizermeeden, Groningen,[4] and Russia.[5] These papers reflect an effort to record basic rain water chemistry with implications for variations due to natural (meteorological) or human (combustion of carbon-based fuels, e.g., wood and coal) influences. Cowling[1] then provides a chronology of increased monitoring of rain water in Europe and North America and to increased research relating the effects of acidification to biotic and abiotic components of the environment.

The decades of the 1950s and 1960s saw a continuation of research dealing with the chemical composition of rain and the atmosphere, and focused on the implications of acidification of rainfall as a result of industrial sources of pollution, predominantly researched during this period in Europe.[6,7] These European research initiatives led to one of the first major general reviews of the phenomenon linking increased acidification of rain and other forms of precipitation attributed to the generation of sulfur dioxide in the industrialized regions of West Germany and England.[8]

John Reuss of the U.S. National Ecology Research Laboratory (Corvallis, Oregon) authored one of the earliest U.S. technical reports linking carbon dioxide–carbonate equilibrium and its relationship to the ecological effects of increased acidity of acid rainfall.[9] In the same year F. B. Hill proposed the need for increased data to more accurately model the impacts of sulfur dioxide and ecosystem responses to environmental dosing of sulfur compounds in the environment.[10] At the close of the 1960s Svante Oden described the effects of changing acidity of precipitation in Sweden as a result of industrial pollutants in England and their transport over space and time and their impacts to the environment.[11] Cowling[1] noted that a series of lectures by Oden at the 1971 International Limnological Congress in Winnipeg, Manitoba, stimulated both scientific and public scrutiny of acid rain and its effects on the North American continent.

The 1970s was marked by a rapid increase in the gathering of preliminary background data and information on the phenomenon of acid rain. As a result of this increase in research and investigation, it was the decade of the 1970s that saw the first trends of a rapid growth in the literature base related to acid(ic) rain and acid(ic) precipitation.[12-17] Publication of the *1st International Symposium on Acid Precipitation and the Forest Ecosystem*[18] held in 1975 coincided with the publication of a triple, special issue of the journal, *Water, Air, and Soil Pollution*,[19] all in 1976, and marked the beginning of a period of rapid growth and accumulation of literature related to acid(ic) rain and acid(ic) precipitation. It was during this period that researchers such as Gene Likens, F. Herbert Borman, and Charles Cogbill[14-17] noted patterns similar to those cited by Oden in rain water chemistry and the environments of North America, especially in the Northeast U.S. and Southeast Canada.

COORDINATED RESEARCH IN THE 1980s

In 1977 the President's Council on Environmental Quality began calling for the consolidation of the existing data-monitoring and research programs such as the National Atmospheric Deposition Program and the Multistate Atmospheric Power Production Pollution Study. President Jimmy Carter announced in August 1979 the creation of a 10-year initiative to study the causes and effects of acid precipitation in Title VII of the Energy Security Act (P.L. 96-264), the Acid Precipitation Act of 1980. A major provision of the Acid Precipitation Act was the creation of the National Acid Precipitation Assessment Program (NAPAP) to define an ongoing, 10-year research initiative to provide a solid scientific understanding for the development of sound environmental policies that were to be needed to address the issues related to acid rain. This initiative was to provide the scientific data and resulting scientific understanding on which environmental policies would be crafted to deal with the problems related to acidification of ecosystems.

It was during the NAPAP era that coordinated interdisciplinary and interagency research was started, and took on its own transboundary aspects with conferences focusing on the international exchange of ideas, resources, and research results. The media increased its news coverage of the phenomenon of acid rain, which until the late 1970s had remained more of an academic or scientific curiosity. As media coverage increased so did public concerns and demands for answers to the issue of acid rain.

This period of coordinated scientific research had the unique feature of providing the scientific and technical underpinnings for the development of policies that would ameliorate, reduce, or otherwise eliminate the threats to the Earth's ecosystems resulting from the effects of acid precipitation. The topic generally called acid rain became the first major transboundary environmental issue where the debate of science-driven policy vs. policy-driven science was carried out very much under public scrutiny. The coordination of research clearly focused on the need for interdisciplinary initiatives involving not only the physical and life sciences, but also the social and policy sciences as well. The relationship between scientific research and policy developments took on new meanings amid the political climate of the 1980s in the U.S. and elsewhere. The generation, management, evaluation and analyses, and sharing of the resulting research and monitoring data were critical.

USE OF DATA FOR CONTINUATION OF A RESEARCH AGENDA AND IMPLEMENTING POLICIES

Authorization of the Clean Air Act Amendments of 1990, including the landmark provisions of the Acidic Deposition Control Program as Title IV of the 1990 Clean Air Act Amendments (Public Law 101-549), was the policy statement crafted after the data-generating activities coordinated by the initial 10-year agenda of NAPAP. The passage of these amendments coincided with the end of the 10-year initial mandate of NAPAP. However, provisions of the Clean Air Act Amendments included continuation of the long-term monitoring and research programs established by NAPAP, as refinements of research agendas and monitoring programs became the driving force of acid rain study into the 21st century.

NAPAP was reauthorized in 1990 to "continue coordination of federal acid deposition research and monitoring of emissions, acidic depositions, and its effects. NAPAP reports to Congress on these activities and assesses the costs, benefits, and effectiveness of the Acidic Deposition Control Program in a form that is useful to policymakers."[20] NAPAP remains as the coordinating office between six federal agencies, and continues to foster cooperation among its members, other governments, states, universities, and the private sector. The participating agencies are the National Oceanic and Atmospheric Administration (NOAA), the Environmental Protection Agency (EPA), the Department of Energy (DOE), the Department of the Interior (DOI), the Department of Agriculture (USDA), and the National Aeronautics and Space Administration (NASA).

ACID RAIN RESEARCH IN THE U.S.– SOURCES OF ENVIRONMENTAL AND ECOLOGICAL DATA

Following is a short and *representative sample* of a few dozen of the hundreds of high-quality acid rain Web sites available for researchers, policy makers, educators, students, librarians, managers, and administrators to use when looking for data and information resources on the topics related to acid rain. These resources were selected for inclusion in this paper due to the long-term commitment of research and data archiving activities undertaken by these research and data-monitoring programs. Over nearly three decades of research and monitoring, these sites serve as major sources of ecological data, and in many cases, their previous and ongoing acid rain-related data gathering represents one of several other types of ecological data (e.g., climatic change, biodiversity, flora and fauna density and distribution, etc.) collected at these sites. Many other acid rain data links are provided by the "other links" compiled by individual institutions, agencies, or facilities described here.

National Acid Precipitation Assessment Program (NAPAP)

http://www.oar.noaa.gov/organization/napap.html

NAPAP remains an interagency program to coordinate scientific research, environmental monitoring, and integrated assessments for examining the effects of acid precursors, sulfur dioxide and oxides of nitrogen. NAPAP's biennial reports provide the scientific underpinnings linking ongoing research and monitoring activities to policy initiatives. In addition to NAPAP's assessment documents and reports is the Tracking and Analysis Framework, a modeling framework developed to access, inform, and guide U.S. regulatory policies on emissions of acid rain precursors. The TAF Model can be navigated by going to its Web site at http://www.lumnia.com/taf/start.htm. Table 1 lists acid rain-specific Web sites maintained by federal departments and agencies participating in NAPAP.

The National Atmospheric Deposition Program/ National Trends Network (NADP/NTN)

http://nadp.sws.uiuc.edu/nadpoverview.asp

NADP/NTN was established in 1978 as a network of twenty-two monitoring stations in the U.S. Today, more than 200 stations are found in the continental U.S., Alaska, Puerto Rico, and the Virgin Islands. In addition to monitoring pre-

TABLE 1. Acid Rain Web Sites for Federal NAPAP or Acid Rain Departments and Agencies.

EPA	http://www.epa.gov/airmarkets/acidrain/
NOAA	**http://www.oar.noaa.gov/organization/napap.html**
	http://www.oar.noaa.gov/atmosphere/
USGS/DOI	http://bqs.usgs.gov/acidrain/

cipitation for hydrogen (acidity as pH), sulfate, nitrate, ammonium, chloride, and base cations (e.g., calcium, magnesium, potassium, and sodium) (Figure 1), more than thirty-five sites are now participating in the Mercury Deposition Network (formed in 1995 to collect weekly samples for mercury content). From this site it is possible to link to a variety of NADP data products:

- Weekly and daily precipitation chemistry data
- Monthly, seasonal, and annual precipitation-weighted mean concentrations
- Annual and seasonal deposition totals
- Mercury deposition data
- Daily precipitation totals
- Color isopleth maps of precipitation concentrations and wet deposition
- Site photos, maps, and descriptive information
- Quality assurance data and information

NADP/NTN data are available for individual sites or as a series of isopleth maps (1994 to 2001 data) as gif images (such as the map for hydrogen ion concentration as measured by pH values collected at the various NADP/NTN field laboratories), animations, and Adobe PDF (portable document format) maps (there are a total of twenty-two maps, one for each parameter): Lab pH, Lab H Deposition (kg/ha), Field pH (pictured in Figure 1–for the year 2001), Field H Deposition (kg/ha), SO_4 Concentrations (mg/L), SO_4 Deposition (kg/ha), NO_3 Concentrations (mg/L), NO_3 Deposition (kg/ha), NH_4 Concentrations (mg/L), NH_4 Deposition (kg/ha), Ca Concentrations (mg/L), Ca Deposition (kg/ha), Mg Concentrations (ug/L), Mg Deposition (kg/ha), K Concentrations (ug/L), K Deposition (kg/ha), Na Concentrations (ug/L), Na Deposition (kg/ha), Cl Concentrations (mg/L), Cl Deposition (kg/ha), N Deposition (from NO3 and NH4) (kg/ha), Measured Precipitation (cm). Map animations from these data are found at: http://nadp.sws.uiuc.edu/amaps/.

The Atmospheric Integrated Research Monitoring Network is part of the NADP/NTN and provides a higher resolution of temporal acid rain data. A variety of AIRMoN data products can be retrieved at http://www.arl.noaa.gov/research/programs/airmon.html. Data provided includes daily wet and dry deposition and various inter-laboratory programs in the U.S. and Canada.

Man and the Biosphere Program (MAB)
http://www.mabnetamericas.org/

The MAB Program represents a worldwide, interdisciplinary research program providing information for a variety of natural resources and environmental issues. As an intergovernmental program, MAB is a showcase for coordinated,

FIGURE 1. The National Atmospheric Deposition Program (NRSP-3)/National Trends Network (NADP/NTN) http://nadp.sws.uiuc.edu/nadpoverview.asp.

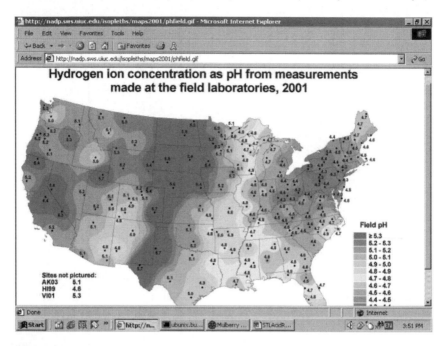

NADP Program Office, Illinois State Water Survey, 2204 Griffith Drive, Champaign, IL 61820. Used with permission.

international cooperation and collaboration for research and monitoring of the Earth's ecosystems.

MAB is an international cooperative of environmental research organizations operating in the following regional networks:

- AfriNet
- ArabNet
- East Asia

- EuroMAB
- MABNetAmericas
- IberoMAB

- USMAB

Biodiversity Resources for Inventorying and Monitoring is a major component of MAB and is a collaboration of U.S. MAB and the Information Center for the Environment to facilitate collection and dissemination of biological inventory and monitoring information derived from protected areas worldwide. Components of BRIM include the MABFlora and MABFauna software programs to standardize methods in the collection, storage, and retrieval of bioinventory information.

The U.S. MAB is operated by the Bureau of Oceans and International Environmental and Scientific Affairs, an agency of the U.S. State Department. A July 1, 1998 directive describes the main functions of biosphere reserves as:

- conservation of important biological resources;
- development of environmentally sound economic growth;
- support of environmental research, monitoring, education, and training;
- as a framework to bring people together to accomplish the above three.

The United States has forty-seven biosphere reserves with ninety-nine administrative units. The *protected areas* and *managed use areas* are owned/administered by the National Park Service; USDA Forest Service; state, county, or city governments; U.S. Fish and Wildlife Service; The Nature Conservancy; universities; private owners; USDA Agricultural Research Service; National Oceanic and Atmospheric Administration; Bureau of Land Management; Tennessee Valley Authority; and the Department of Energy. U.S. Biosphere Reserves, including their locations and sponsoring agencies, are appended to this paper. Each Biosphere Reserve maintains its own research and monitoring networks, programs, and services, and is responsible for its site's data and information management and sharing strategies.

One such U.S. Biosphere Reserve is managed by the Adirondack Park Agency (APA). The Champlain-Adirondack Biosphere Reserve is a major source of acid rain data and information related to the largest protected wilderness area in the contiguous United States (http://www.northnet.org/adirondackparkagency/). The APA oversees the research and monitoring activities within the Adirondack Park, including a growing body of GIS coverage, that now includes maps, land use data, legal jurisdictions and land designations, and wetlands designations. Much of this GIS data is now available from the APA in CD-ROM format.

Influences on Wetlands and Lakes in the Adirondack Park of New York State–A Catalog of Existing and New GIS Data Layers for the 400,000 Hectare Oswegatchie/Black River Watershed is one of the specific Adirondack Park reports which includes access to data related to ongoing acid rain monitoring. The following data layers are divided into thematic groups as they appear on the final report poster. Links for each data layer lead to a graphic image of the data, to the topic in the final report, metadata when available, and to other related documents.

- *Vegetative Cover*
  - Upland Cover from TM Data
  - Wetlands

- *Geology/Soils*
  - Bedrock Geology
  - Surficial Geology
  - Bedrock Acid Neutralizing Capacity
  - General Soils–Parent Material
  - Elevation

- *Land Use*
  - Adirondack Park Land Use & Development Plan
  - 1989 Residential Areas

- *Hydrology/Atmospheric*
  - Watersheds and Adirondack Long Term Monitoring Waters
  - Mean Annual Precipitation (1951 to 1980)
  - Total Nitrogen Deposition

- *Landscape Disturbance*
  - State Forest Acquisition
  - 1916 Fire Protection
  - November 1950 Blowdown
  - Forest Damage Assessment of July 1995 Blowdown
  - Landscape Disturbance Composite (to 1950)

The APA has worked closely with the New York State Department of Environmental Conservation in conducting one of the major acid rain monitoring projects in the U.S. An ongoing monitoring network was established and continued by the Adirondack Lakes Survey Corporation (ALSC). ALSC is a not-for-profit corporation established in 1984 as a cooperative agreement between the Empire State Electric Energy Research Corporation and the New York State Department of Environmental Conservation to monitor the extent and magnitude of acidification of lakes and ponds in the Adirondack region. ALSC continues to obtain and provide monitoring data to researchers, policy makers, educators, and others (Figure 2). Presently, the ALSC receives joint funding from the New York State Energy Research and Development Authority (NYSERDA) and the U.S. EPA. Data available include physical attributes of wetland and watershed areas, data about the 1950 blowdown (resulting in excessive forest damage), the 1916 wild fires, the 1995 miroburst wind storm that ravaged large portions of the western Adirondack region, various land use data, bedrock and surficial geologic data, soil parameters, and atmospheric data (precipitation, nitrate and sulfate data). These data are provided in polygon and raster format for GIS coverages.

FIGURE 2. Various data are available from the Adirondack Lakes Survey Corporation, which collected, analyzed, and archived one of the largest and highest resolution (geographically) data sets of the Adirondack Region of New York State.

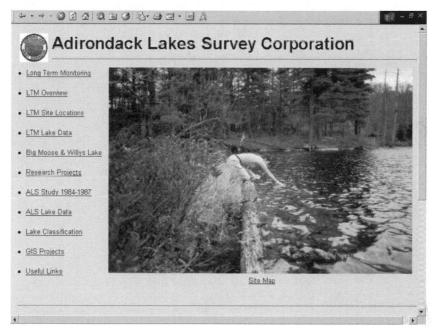

Used with permission.

The ALCS's acid rain monitoring began with an extensive baseline survey conducted from 1984-1987 and culminated with the publication of a 1990 Adirondack Lakes Survey Report (http://www.adirondacklakessurvey.org/execsum.htm). Since that time, acid rain monitoring surveys, fisheries and watershed projects have continued with the most intensive of these being the Long-Term Monitoring Project (http://www.adirondacklakessurvey. org/ltmpage.htm) that began in June 1992 and continues presently. A special highlight of this Web site is the month-by-month chemistry update for two key monitoring lakes, Big Moose Lake and Willys Lake (http://www. adirondacklakessurvey.org/monthly.html). The *Adirondack Lakes Survey: 1987 Report* is a 3-volume set of data collected in the Lower Hudson River region.

The original *Adirondack Lakes Survey* is a 19-volume set of the original 1984-1989 monitoring activities where extensive data were collected in hundreds of Adirondack lakes and ponds and select waters in the Hudson River watershed. The following data were collected for each lake tested: location and status, bathymetric map, morphometrics, macroinvertebrate macrophytes, fisheries, chemical/physical parameters, and management history arranged by numerical listing of lakes within each major Adirondack watershed. An additional three volumes were added in 1989 for watersheds of the Lower Hudson River. In all, these Adirondack data represent about twenty linear shelf-feet of loose-leaf datasheets. As mentioned above only small sets of these data have been converted into CD-ROM or other electronic formats. Conversion of print data is contingent on the availability of funding.

Long Term Ecological Research (LTER) Network
http://lternet.edu

LTER is another collaborative research effort that links more than 1,100 scientists and students in ongoing investigations of ecological processes covering long-term temporal scales and broad geographic scales. The LTER was established in 1980 by the National Science Foundation to support dedicated, long-term ecological research in the U.S. There are 24 LTER sites in the U.S. (Figure 3):

- Andrews LTER
- Arctic Tundra LTER
- Baltimore Ecosystem Study
- Bonanza Creek LTER
- Central Arizona–Phoenix
- Cedar Creek LTER
- Coweeta LTER
- Harvard Forest
- Hubbard Brook LTER
- Jornada Basin
- Kellogg Biological Station
- Konza LTER
- Luquillo LTER
- McMurdo Dry Valleys
- Niwot Ridge LTER
- North Temperate Lakes
- Palmer Station
- Plum Island Ecosystem
- Sevilleta LTER
- Shortgrass Steppe
- Virginia Coast Reserve
- Florida Coastal Everglades
- Georgia Coastal Ecosystems
- Santa Barbara Coastal

As with the U.S. MAB Biosphere Reserves, each LTER site should be examined for its own research, monitoring, and data and information management activities and data-sharing policies. You will note that there is an overlap in the reporting jurisdictions of the LTER Network Sites and the U.S. MAB Biosphere Preserves, such as is the case with the Hubbard Brook Ecological Study (HBES) site.

Among the LTER sites, The Hubbard Brook Ecosystem Study <http://www.hubbardbrook.org/> facility is, perhaps, the best known for its comprehensive and pioneering acid rain research. HBES is a long-term ecological research project located at the Hubbard Brook Experimental Forest (HBEF), a 3,160

FIGURE 3. This map shows the location of all 24 LTER sites at http://lternet. edu/sites.

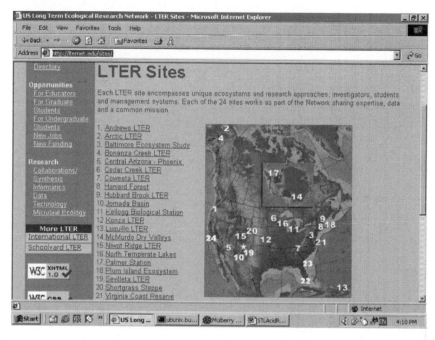

Image courtesy of the LTER Network Office.

hectare reserve located in the White Mountain National Forest, near North Woodstock, New Hampshire. The HBEF, also a USMAB site, was established by the USDA Forest Service in 1955 as a major center for hydrologic research in New England. A large repository of "Research and Data" is available from its Web site (Figure 4) and presents a description of long-term data sets and the on-site research activities of the HBES:

- Stream Flow and Chemistry
- Atmospheric Inputs (precipitation and deposition)
- Vegetation
- Weather and Climate Data
- Watershed Budgets
- Soil Conditions and Chemistry
- Animals
- Lake Chemistry
- Paleoecology

FIGURE 4. The Hubbard Brook Experimental Forest in the White Mountains of New Hampshire is part of the LTER network. Researchers have been investigating the impacts of increased acidification to forested ecosystems for nearly 40 years at the HBEF. Examples of the types of research data available can be located from a Hubbard Brook Web site http://www.hubbardbrook.org/research/ research.htm.

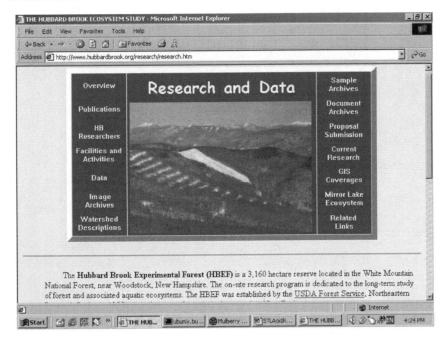

Used with permission.

Data are provided in print/hard copy reports and publications as well as online data files and data sets. Images (photographs, aerial photos, and graphics), GIS coverages, and publications are also provided by the HBES.

Current and ongoing ecological research at Hubbard Brook reveals new initiatives, concerns, and topical interests that may have been spawned from the initial studies of acidification on the resident ecosystem. These new areas of research, listed by disciplinary interest, reflect an ongoing and prolific generation of ecological and environmental data from this single LTER location (other LTER sites also have extensive ecological data holdings):

- *Vegetation Studies*
  - Long-term changes in the calcium concentration of wood fern fronds

- Regional Sugar Maple Study
- Spatial patterns of tree species abundance
- Species-specific trace element uptake in trees
- Single tree biomass calculator

- *Soil and Soil Biota Research*
  - Studies of Fungi at Hubbard Brook
  - Detrital Foodwebs in northern hardwood forest soils
  - A Spatial Model of Soil Parent Material
  - Accumulation and Depletion of Base Cations in Forest Floors
  - Forest Floor Organic Matter following Logging in Northern Hardwoods
  - Is there missing S at the HBEF?

- *Hydrology Research*
  - Increasing Atmospheric CO_2 and Forest Water Use

- *Geology and Geochemistry Research*
  - The bedrock geology of the Hubbard Brook Experimental Forest: Results of new 1:10,000 mapping
  - Characterizing fractured rock hydrology in the Mirror Lake Watershed
  - Effects of landscape position and forest type on mineral weathering

ADDITIONAL INTERNET WEB SITES
FOR DATA AND INFORMATION RESOURCES

U.S. DATA TABLES: Actual acid rain data for official U.S. testing stations can be found at: http://nadp.nrel.colostate.edu/NAD. Click on a state to find the most comprehensive data available anywhere. By entering a time period you can find the official readings from the site closest to you by the week.

Walker Branch Watershed: Sponsored by the U.S. Department of Energy's Office of Health and Environmental Research, Biological and Environmental Research operated by the Environmental Sciences Division at Oak Ridge National Laboratory (ORNL), and the Atmospheric Turbulence and Diffusion Division, Air Resources Laboratory, National Oceanic and Atmospheric Administration in Oak Ridge, Tennessee. Data holdings are archived at http://www.esd.ornl.gov/programs/WBW/, including the Walker Branch data reported to the NADP/NTN at: http://nadp.sws.uiuc.edu/sites/siteinfo.asp?id=TN00&net=NADP.

U.S. CURRENT pH MAP: You can view a map of the most current acid rain data inventories (latest is for November 26 to December 23, 2001) at: http://water.usgs.gov/nwc/NWC/pH/html/ph.html.

CANADA: Canadian acid rain data can be viewed at: http://www.ns.ec. gc.ca/msc/as/as_acid.html.

EUROPEAN FORESTS: Maps showing acid rain damage to European forests can be found at: http://www.soton.ac.uk/~engenvir/environment/air/ acid.how.big.problem.html.

PENNSYLVANIA ATMOSPHERIC DEPOSITION MONITORING NETWORK (PADMN) has provided the results of statewide monitoring data since 1981, and now includes mercury (Hg) deposition monitoring data since 1997 at: http://www.dep.state.pa.us/dep/deputate/airwaste/aq/acidrain/acidrain.htm.

NORWAY: Maps showing increasing acid rain-induced damage to Norway's rivers are at: http://www.grida.no/soeno95/acidrain/effects.htm.

CONCLUSIONS

Data related to acid rain will continue to increase in future decades as long-term research and monitoring projects continue. The rate of growth of acid rain data will decrease in volume over the years, as research initiatives begun more than a quarter of a century ago come to close and as monitoring programs are incorporated into more broadly defined global environmental change and integrated assessment programs, such as those outlined at Oak Ridge National Laboratory,[21] including comprehensive data collections provided by the Carbon Dioxide Information Analysis Center at their Web site, http://cdiac.esd.ornl.gov/, and its co-located World Data Center for Atmospheric Trace Gases http://www. ngdc.noaa.gov/wdc/wdca/wdca_atmosgas.html.

Access to real-time, on-demand data related to all aspects of acid rain science and policy will continue to be rigorously pursued, and the growth of such data repositories will increase and become more organized. Digitization of historical data will continue at its present painfully slow place unless funding and technical support is provided for such print-to-electronic conversions to take place, especially for monitoring program data collected by state agencies or supported by subnational agencies and institutions.

Data will continue to be collected at the various ecological and environmental research and monitoring sites listed. The issue of acid rain paved a two- to three-decades long (or longer) data collection that is evolving into data resources for a host of other ecological and environmental topics. Keeping abreast of the individual and collective activities of these institutions is a challenge for researchers, educators, and librarians and other information and data providers. The networks described here provide starting points from which to begin.

REFERENCES

1. Cowling, Ellis B. 1982. Acid precipitation in historical perspective. *Environmental Science and Technology*, 16(2): 110A-123A.

2. Anderson, V.G. 1915. Influence of Weather conditions on amounts of nitric acid and of nitrous acid in the rainfall near Melbourne, Australia. *Quarterly Journal of the Royal Meteorological Society*, 41: 99-122.

3. Gerlach, R. 1914. *Proof of the origin of smoke acids in rain-water flowing down tree trunks by means of an automatic separator and the influence of these acids on the soil.* Experimental Station Record, 32: 422.

4. Hudig, J. 1912. The amount of nitrogen as ammonia and nitric acid (and nitrous) acid in the rain water collected at Uithuizermeeden, Groningen. *Journal of Agricultural Science*, 4: 260-69.

5. Vituynii, I. 1912. Amounts of chlorine and sulfuric acid in rain water. *Journal of the Chemical Society, Abstracts*, 100(II): 432 and *Journal fuer Experimentelle Landwirthschaft*, 12, 20-30 (Russian); Abstract: 30-2 (German).

6. Witt, Ernst. 1969. Lethal effect of exhaust gases on the water fauna. *Zentralblatt fuer Arbeitsmedizin Arbeitsschutz*, 19(9): 264-65.

7. Nyberg, Alf. 1970. Weather changes important for the acidity of rainfall. (*Sweden*). *Forskning och Framsteg*, 1: 18-21.

8. Reiquam, H. 1970. European Interest in acidic precipitation. Review. *AEC Symposium Series*, 22: 289-92.

9. Reuss, John O. 1975. *Chemical-biological Relations Relevant to Ecological Effects of Acid Rainfall.* NTIS Report PB-244409, National Ecological Research Laboratory, Environmental Protection Agency, EPA-660-3-75-032 53.

10. Hill. F.B. 1975. *Some Information Needs for Air Quality Modeling*, CONF-750572-1. Brookhaven National Laboratory, Upton, NY. Report BNL-25041.

11. Oden, S. 1968. *The Acidification of Air and Precipitation and Its Consequences in the Natural Environment, Ecology Committee Bulletin*, No. 1. Stockholm, Sweden: Swedish National Science Research Council.

12. Beamish, Richard J. 1972. Acidification of the La Cloche Mountain Lakes, Ontario, and resulting fish mortalities. *Journal of the Fisheries Research Board of Canada*, 29(8): 1131-43.

13. Askne, C. and Brosset, C. 1972. Determination of strong acid in precipitation, lake water, and airbourne matter. *Atmospheric Environment*, 6(9): 695-96.

14. Likens, Gene E., Bormann, F. Herbert, and Johnson, Noye M. 1972. Acid rain. *Environment*, 14(2): 33-40.

15. Likens, Gene E. and Bormann, F. Herbert. Acid rain: Serious regional environmental problem. *Science*, 184(4142): 1176-79.

16. Cogbill, Charles V. and Likens, Gene E. 1974. Acid precipitation in the northeastern United States. *Water Resources Research*, 10(6): 1133-37.

17. Fairfax, J.A.W. and Lepp, N.W. 1975. *Nature* (London), 255(5506): 324-25.

18. Dochinger, L.S. and Seliga, T.A., Eds. 1976. Proceedings of the 1st International Symposium on Acid Precipitation and the Forest Ecosystem, Columbus, Ohio, 1974. Published by the U.S. Department of Agriculture, Forest Service, General Technical Report NE-23, 1074.

19. *Water, Air, and Soil Pollution*, 6(2-3-4), 1976. Special issue devoted to acid rain research.

20. National Acid Precipitation Assessment Program Home Page. National Oceanic and Atmospheric Administration, Silver Spring, Maryland. http://www.oar.noaa.gov/organization/napap.html, Accessed 29 July 2003.

21. Renshaw, Amanda W., Ed. 1995. Integrated Assessment Briefs. ORNL Publication Number ORNL/M-4227. Center for Global Environmental Studies, Oak Ridge National Laboratory, Oak Ridge, Tenn., see also: http://www.ornl.gov/CGES/AFinding.

APPENDIX. U.S. Man and the Biosphere Preserves and Their Sponsoring Agencies

Individual points of contact and Internet information for the U.S. MAB sites is found at http://www.mabnetamericas.org/misc/uscontact.html, the official "U.S. Biosphere Reserves Directory." Each of these preserves maintains its own data collection policies and management strategies, including those policies and protocols for sharing their data with others.

Key: NPS   National Park Service, Department of Interior
  NOAA   National Oceanic and Atmospheric Administration, Department of Commerce
  FWS   U.S. Fish & Wildlife Service, Department of Interior
  FS   Forest Service, Department of Agriculture
  ARS   Agricultural Research Service, Department of Agriculture
  DOE   Department of Energy
  BLM   Bureau of Land Management, Department of Interior
  Private Denotes Some Form of Private Ownership
  Complex Denotes Multiple Ownership

- Aleutian Islands National Wildlife Refuge (FWS)
- Beaver Creek Experimental Watershed (FS)
- Big Bend National Park (NPS)
- Big Thicket National Preserve (NPS)
- California Coast Ranges Biosphere Reserve (8 Units)

  - Elder Creek Area of Critical Environmental Concern (BLM)
  - Heath and Marjorie Angelo Coast Range Preserve (University of California)
  - Jackson Demonstration State Forest (California Department of Forests)
  - Landels-Hill Big Creek Reserve (University of California)

- Redwood Experimental Forest (FS)
- Redwood National Park (NPS)
- North Coast Redwoods District State Parks (3 Units)
  - Del Norte Coast Redwoods State Park and Alternate Site (California Department of Parks and Recreation)
  - Jebediah Smith Redwoods State Park and Alternate Site (California Department of Parks and Recreation)
  - Prairie Creek Redwoods State Park and Alternate Site (California Department of Parks and Recreation)
  - Western Slopes of Cone Peak, Los Padres National Forest (FS)
- Carolinian-South Atlantic Biosphere Reserve (11 Units)
  - Blackbeard Island and Wolf Island National Wildlife Refuges (FWS)
  - Cape Lookout National Seashore (NPS)
  - Cape Romain National Wildlife Refuge (FWS)
  - Capers Island Heritage Preserve (South Carolina Department of Natural Resources, Marine Resources Division)
  - Cumberland Island National Seashore (NPS)
  - Gray's Reef National Marine Sanctuary (NOAA)
  - Hobcaw Barony (North Inlet) (Complex Private)
  - Little St. Simons Island (Private)
  - Santee Coastal Reserve (South Carolina Department of Natural Resources)
  - Washo Reserve (The Nature Conservancy)
  - Tom Yawkey Wildlife Center (South Carolina Department of Natural Resources)
- Cascade Head Experimental Forest & Scenic Research Area (FS)
- Central California Coast Biosphere Reserve (See Golden Gate Biosphere Reserve)
- Central Gulf Coastal Plain Biosphere Reserve
  - Apalachicola National Estuarine Research Reserve and Alternate Site (NOAA)
- Central Plains Experimental Range (ARS)
- Champlain-Adirondack Biosphere Reserve (3 Units)
  - Adirondack Park Agency (Private)
  - Green Mountain National Forest (FS)
  - Mount Mansfield State Natural Area (Vermont Agency of Natural Resources)
- Channel Islands Biosphere Reserve (2 Units)
  - Channel Islands National Park (NPS)
  - Channel Islands National Marine Sanctuary (NOAA)

- Coram Experimental Forest (FS)
- Denali National Park and Biosphere Reserve (NPS)
- Desert Experimental Range (ARS)
- Everglades National Park (with Dry Tortugas National Park) (NPS)
- Fraser Experimental Forest (FS)
- Glacier Bay-Admiralty Island Biosphere Reserve (2 Units)
    - Admiralty Island National Monument (FS)
    - Glacier Bay National Park and Preserve (NPS)
- Glacier National Park (NPS)
- Golden Gate Biosphere Reserve (13 Units)
    - Bolinas Lagoon Preserve and Cypress Grove Preserve (Private)
    - Bodega Marine Reserve (University of California)
    - Cordell Bank National Marine Sanctuary (NOAA)
    - Farallon National Wildlife Refuge (FWS)
    - Golden Gate National Recreation Area (NPS)
    - Gulf of the Farallones National Marine Sanctuary (NOAA)
    - Jasper Ridge Biological Preserve (Coordinator) (Stanford University)
    - Marin Municipal Water District (Marin County, California)
    - Mount Tamalpais State Park (California Department of Parks and Recreation)
    - Point Reyes National Seashore (NPS)
    - San Francisco Peninsular Watershed (City of San Francisco, California)
    - Tomales Bay State Park (California Department of Parks and Recreation)
    - Samuel P. Taylor State Park (California Department of Parks and Recreation)
- Guanica Commonwealth Forest Reserve (Puerto Rico Department of Natural Resources)
- Hawaiian Islands Biosphere Reserve (2 Units)
    - Hawaiian Volcanoes National Park (NPS)
    - Haleakala National Park (NPS)
- H. J. Andrews Experimental Forest (FS)
- Hubbard Brook Experimental Forest (FS)
- Isle Royale National Park (NPS)
- Jornada Experimental Range (ARS)
- Konza Prairie Research Natural Area (The Nature Conservancy)
- Land Between the Lakes (Tennessee Valley Authority)
- Luquillo Experimental Forest (FS)
- Mammoth Cave Area and Barren River Area Development District, BRADD (NPS and Complex)

- Mojave and Colorado Deserts Biosphere Reserve (5 Units)
    - Anza-Borrego Desert State Park and Alternate Site (California Department of Parks and Recreation)
    - Death Valley National Monument (NPS)
    - Joshua Tree National Monument (NPS)
    - Philip L. Boyd Deep Canyon Desert Center (University of California)
    - Santa Rosa Wildlife Management Area, San Bernadino National Forest (FS)
- New Jersey Pinelands Biosphere Reserve (Pinelands Commission, Complex)
- Niwot Ridge Biosphere Reserve (University of Colorado)
- Noatak National Preserve (2 Units)
    - Gates of the Arctic National Park (NPS)
    - Noatak National Preserve (NPS)
- Olympic National Park (NPS)
- Organ Pipe Cactus National Monument (NPS)
- Rocky Mountain National Park (NPS)
- San Dimas Experimental Forest (FS)
- San Joaquin Experimental Range (ARS)
- Sequoia-Kings Canyon National Parks (NPS)
- South Atlantic Coastal Plain Biosphere Reserve
- Congaree Swamp National Monument (NPS)
- Southern Appalachian Biosphere Reserve (5 Units)
    - Coweeta Hydrologic Laboratory (FS)
    - Grandfather Mountain (Private)
    - Great Smoky Mountains National Park (NPS)
    - Mt. Mitchell State Park (North Carolina Department of Environmental Health and Natural Resources)
    - Oak Ridge National Environmental Research Park (DOE)
- Stanislaus-Tuolumne Experimental Forest (FS)
- Three Sisters Wilderness, Deschutes National Forest (FS)
- University of Michigan Biological Station (University of Michigan)
- Virgin Islands National Park and Biosphere Reserve (NPS)
- Virginia Coast Reserve (The Nature Conservancy)
- Yellowstone National Park (NPS)

Information Science
and Technology Developments
Within the National Biological
Information Infrastructure

Michael T. Frame
Gladys Cotter
Lisa Zolly
Janice Little

SUMMARY. Whether your vantage point is that of an office window or a national park, your view undoubtedly encompasses a rich diversity of life forms, all carefully studied or managed by some scientist, resource manager, or planner. A few simple calculations–the number of species, their interrelationships, and the many researchers studying them–and you can easily see the tremendous challenges that the resulting biological data presents to the information and computer science communities. Biological information varies in format and content: it may pertain to a particular species or an entire ecosystem; it can contain land use characteristics, and

Michael T. Frame (E-mail: Mike_frame@usgs.gov), Gladys Cotter (E-mail: Gladys_cotter@usgs.gov), and Lisa Zolly (E-mail: Lisa_zolly@usgs.gov) are all affiliated with the U.S. Geological Survey, 302 National Center, Reston, VA 20192. Janice Little is affiliated with the U.S. Geological Survey, Denver Federal Center, Denver, CO 80225 (E-mail: Janice_little@usgs.gov).

[Haworth co-indexing entry note]: "Information Science and Technology Developments Within the National Biological Information Infrastructure." Frame, Michael T. et al. Co-published simultaneously in *Science & Technology Libraries* (The Haworth Information Press, an imprint of The Haworth Press, Inc.) Vol. 23, No. 4, 2003, pp. 59-72; and: *Online Ecological and Environmental Data* (ed: Virginia Baldwin) The Haworth Information Press, an imprint of The Haworth Press, Inc., 2003, pp. 59-72. Single or multiple copies of this article are available for a fee from The Haworth Document Delivery Service [1-800-HAWORTH, 9:00 a.m. - 5:00 p.m. (EST). E-mail address: docdelivery@haworthpress.com].

geospatially referenced information. The complexity and uniqueness of each individual species or ecosystem do not easily lend themselves to today's computer science tools and applications. To address the challenges that the biological enterprise presents, the National Biological Information Infrastructure (NBII) (http://www.nbii.gov) was established in 1993 on the recommendation of the National Research Council (National Research Council 1993). The NBII is designed to address these issues on a national scale, and through international partnerships. This paper discusses current information and computer science efforts within the National Biological Information Infrastructure Program, and future computer science research endeavors that are needed to address the ever-growing issues related to our nation's biological concerns. *[Article copies available for a fee from The Haworth Document Delivery Service: 1-800-HAWORTH. E-mail address: <docdelivery@haworthpress.com> Website: <http://www.HaworthPress.com> © 2003 by The Haworth Press, Inc. All rights reserved.]*

KEYWORDS. Bio-informatics, National Biological Information Infrastructure, biology, distributed networks, intelligent agents

INTRODUCTION

The National Biological Information Infrastructure (NBII) is a broad, collaborative program designed to provide increased access to data and information on the Nation's biological resources. The NBII links diverse, high-quality biological databases, information products, and analytical tools maintained by NBII partners and other contributors in government agencies, academic institutions, non-government organizations, and private industry. NBII partners and collaborators also work on new standards, tools, and technologies that make it easier to find, integrate, and apply biological resources information. Resource managers, scientists, educators, and the general public use the NBII to answer a wide range of questions related to the management, use, or conservation of this Nation's biological resources.

THE CHALLENGES OF BIOLOGICAL INFORMATION

Biodiversity data are collected by a variety of organizations within the U.S. for purposes of scientific understanding and natural resource management. Scientific enquiry includes studies that are carried out by educational institutions, museums, and zoos. These institutions are funded through private organizations or the government and provide a wealth of data used to address basic scientific questions related to biodiversity. The information and knowledge derived are made available through the peer-review process and provide much of the foundational understanding of biodiversity. Decisions regarding the availability of the resulting data are based upon a variety of criteria, including personal preference; organizational policies; availability of funds; technological capabilities for storage and access; and commercialization potential. The length of time that the data will be made available is also subject to a similar set of criteria, including longevity of both the storage medium and the technology used to store the data sets; the institution's archival policies; funding to support the maintenance of the archive; and the potential long-term financial value of the data. Clearly, the physical and temporal aspects of access are key issues for biological information.

In addition to institutionally owned biodiversity data, similar data arc collected under the auspices of various governmental bodies. The scope and scale of the data varies, but is often targeted to local issues such as land use planning, or invasive or endangered species. In addition, there are numerous data collection activities at regional and national levels, with little or no national coordinated integration between these levels or with the more localized data collections (President's Committee of Advisors on Science and Technology Panel on Biodiversity and Ecosystems 1998). Data therefore exists in disparate formats, at varying scales, on servers that may or may not be accessible, or even known, by other researchers. Costly duplication of efforts, loss of collaborative opportunities, and the unknown existence of key data holdings are only some of the persistent failings associated with remotely held data collections. An additional thought to consider: local and Federal government agencies are likely funding agents for the basic science discussed above (Fornwall 2003).

The NBII is addressing these information and computer science issues, and related policies, within the United States as well as internationally, through its various organizational and technological partnerships. These challenges have resulted in the development of several NBII tools and services that have greatly aided users in the creation, discovery, management, and delivery of their information. Five of the major tools are briefly described later in this article.

While the NBII unites hundreds of quality resources from many life sciences disciplines, it traditionally has provided singular access to them; users must examine resources one at a time. In other words, while the NBII offers resources highly pertinent to the information needs of the life sciences and natural resources communities, it nevertheless requires a human agent to determine the relevancy of those resources to a particular information need. The NBII can often mitigate the critical first step for the information needs of scientists:

identification of existing, pertinent data. The discovery of these resources will continue as a critical function of the NBII; however, the NBII must do more to fully meet the resource needs of the scientific community.

· *MEETING THE CHALLENGE: A NEXT-GENERATION NBII*

These needs, articulated by national academies of science, presidential committees, and natural resource management organizations, include back-end solutions such as highly specific relevancy-ranking algorithms, data synthesis capabilities, and analysis. NBII user communities are calling for a commitment to continue development of the NBII through creation of an NBII-2, or next-generation NBII. A 1998 report from the President's Committee of Advisors on Science and Technology (PCAST) entitled "Teaming with Life: Investing in Science to Understand and Use America's Living Capital" (President's Committee of Advisors on Science and Technology Panel on Biodiversity and Ecosystems 1998) stated:

> The economic prosperity and, indeed, the fate of human societies are inextricably linked to the natural world. Because of this, information about biodiversity and ecosystems is vital to a wide range of scientific, education, commercial, and governmental uses. Unfortunately, most of this information exists in forms that are not easily used. . . . There exists no comprehensive technological or organizational framework that allows this information to be readily accessed or used effectively by scientists, resource managers, policy makers, or other potential client communities.

To address this challenge, the NBII initiated funding and development of interconnected data and information "Nodes." A Node is a collection of data, information, tools, or knowledge within a specific geographic region or thematic discipline. In 2001, the NBII established NBII Regional, Thematic, and Infrastructure Nodes (Figure 1).

- *Regional*–Information systems that serve the data and resource needs and issues of a particular geographic region with ecosystem or natural resources commonalities. These Nodes also provide analytical capabilities, technology support, training, and education within the region and depending on capabilities, to the overall NBII enterprise. Examples include the Pacific Basin Information Node (invasive species; coral reefs);

the Southern Appalachian Information Node (cooperative land use planning); the Pacific Northwest Information Node (sustainable forestry; forest management); the California Information Node (invasive species; watershed assessments); the Northern Rockies Information Node (human impacts on wildlife ecosystems); and the Central Southwest/Gulf Coast Information Node (sustainable development).

- *Thematic*–Information systems to address national-level priorities and crosscutting themes related to natural resources management or areas of biological concern. Examples include the Bird Conservation Node (national dissemination and synthesis of major datasets and information related to North American birds); the Fisheries and Aquatic Resources Node (national fish-strain registries; multi-watershed integration of datasets and mapping capabilities); and the Invasive Species Node (dataset integration, GIS capabilities, and decision-support systems for the prevention, management and eradication of terrestrial and aquatic invasive species).
- *Infrastructure*–Collaboratives to develop the tools, technologies, and innovations to significantly enhance the abilities of both information providers and users to identify, retrieve, evaluate, and integrate relevant data and information products for natural resources decision-making. Examples include the Knowledge Integration Node (application of controlled vocabularies to enhance information retrieval); and the Network Standards and Technology Node (evaluation and implementation of existing standards and technologies, and development of system-specific ones, to facilitate integrated information retrieval for a range of products and services–for example, the development of XML-based DTD for information interoperability and retrieval from various distributed data sources).

BioBot–
"INTELLIGENT AGENT FOR THE BIOLOGICAL COMMUNITY"

Due to the rapid growth of electronically accessible content from the Internet, there is a corresponding increase in demand for biological information of all types. And although the World Wide Web presents tremendous opportunities to users for access to a wealth of information, the quantity of that information can be overwhelming. The user who attempts to find information on a particular species, a biological concern, or simply educational information can become confounded by the sheer volume of data and information returned as "pertinent"

FIGURE 1. NBII-2 Nodes

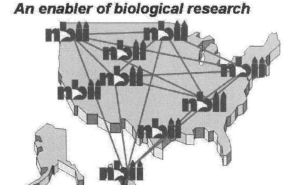

to a user's need. In addition, current awareness becomes an obstacle, as variations in search engine crawls of the Web, as well as the user's own ability to keep up with frequent queries to multiple search tools, can prevent timely access to and knowledge of pertinent information. To address these challenges, the NBII has developed an intelligent agent to harvest and deliver this information.

BioBot is designed to help users in a number of biological data discovery areas, including profiling or defining the information of interest, accessing specific information, and ultimately delivering the needed biological information to a user's desktop. *BioBot* targets the NBII collection, major search engines and indexes, and specific biological collections on the Web to return more relevant search results to users. *BioBot* provides users with the capability to access seamlessly current biological holdings of major sources on the Internet, through a *single* interface.

BioBot users have the option of using the tool for a one-time search on a particular query, or setting up a free "MyNBIIFilter" account to enact a current awareness service for a particular query. In the latter case, an NBII user interested in receiving information on "biodiversity issues in Colorado," as it becomes available on the Web can simply define a query "profile," such as "biodiversity AND Colorado," within *BioBot*. The user then selects the Web resources for *BioBot* to target, followed by the frequency with which *BioBot* should initiate a fresh search on that query. *BioBot* then scours those resources selected by the user, and delivers pertinent sites to the user's "account," a personal Web page on the *BioBot* server. The user can view immediately the initial search results. Afterward, *BioBot* will notify the user by a brief e-mail when it locates *new* sites that match the user's query. The frequency of *BioBot*'s crawls and resulting notification of new information are determined by the user when the query profile is built, and can be set as often as daily, or as seldom as monthly.

Figure 2 depicts a typical *BioBot* profile setup by a user who has multiple current awareness searches active.

Users can select not only their favorite search engines, including the NBII Search engine, but can also choose the query structure most appropriate for them, including simple, Boolean, or Phrase type searches. *BioBot* automatically eliminates duplicate links returned by the selected searching resources, and can verify that retrieved links are "live," all in a matter of seconds. Returned results are stored on a user's account page in an additive fashion; previous search results remain until the user marks them as no longer relevant, and they are deleted when the user logs out of the session. New links are clearly marked for rapid identification. At any time, a user can edit a query profile to restructure a query statement, add or delete Web resources to be searched, and change the interval at which the current awareness search is enacted.

Figure 3 demonstrates some of the capabilities within *BioBot*.

Another feature of *BioBot* is its ability to interact with other existing NBII biological repositories. The need to provide multiple paths to related biological information, regardless of the user's particular entry point in the realm of Web-based information, is paramount to improving information discovery and delivery to users.

One of the most important infrastructure systems within the NBII is the Integrated Taxonomic Information System (ITIS), a scientifically credible and

FIGURE 2. *BioBot* Query Profiles

MyNBIIFilter Home Page

Options: Add Query | Delete All | Help | Sign Off

	Query String	Edit Options	View Results	Delete Query	Rerun Now
1	invasive species	Edit	View	Delete	Rerun
2	zebra mussel	Edit	View	Delete	Rerun
3	Colorado AND biodiversity	Edit	View	Delete	Rerun
4	spotted owl	Edit	View	Delete	Rerun

FIGURE 3. *BioBot* Search Agent Query Menu

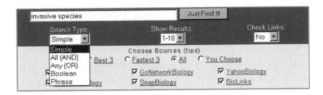

dynamic biological names thesaurus for North American species. Much of the scientific and technical data relating to the natural world includes references to the scientific and/or vernacular names of the species or higher taxonomic groups that are represented in the data. Biological names are thus the common denominator that can be used to link data from many distributed sources and across disciplines, from molecular biology and genetics to entire ecosystem-level studies. Using both scientific and vernacular names within a search query can broaden returned search results, and, perhaps more importantly, can offer the potential for discovery of more *relevant* datasets than does a search on a single form of the species name.

Currently, the *BioBot* search agent is an integrated component of the ITIS. Within ITIS, users can take returned taxonomic information into *BioBot* automatically, simply by selecting the *BioBot* button. Soon, *BioBot* users will be able to select ITIS directly from the main *BioBot* filter page, a service that will eliminate the need to physically access the ITIS system for taxonomic information. The relative effectiveness of this approach versus more conventional strategies is shown in Figure 4.

Figure 4 describes a query from the ITIS system, which then automatically passes all synonyms for either the common name or scientific name of the species. The final screen-shot shows the resulting authoritative and integrated information source.

As one can easily see, *BioBot* is designed to take advantage of the distributed nature of the diverse biological repositories that exist within the National Biological Information Infrastructure Program.

FIGURE 4. Species Integration

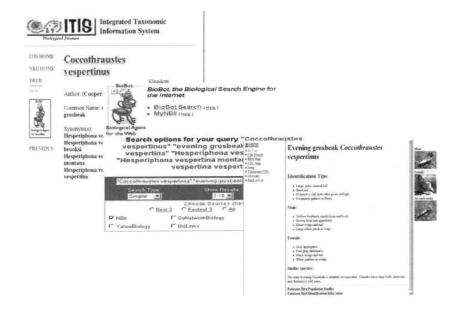

NBII AND META-TAGS

Another effort underway within the NBII Program is comprehensive meta-tags implementation across the NBII network. The use of meta-tags not only boost a site's search engine results ranking–therefore increasing the likelihood that users will find that particular site–but also provide a foundation for future exploitation by more sophisticated search engines that will enable improved information retrieval and discovery on the World Wide Web. Ultimately, the NBII will benefit from the improved access and delivery of biological information to our customers, partners, and stakeholders.

The NBII has developed a list of meta-tags for our partners to implement on their biological information repositories or Web sites. Most of the mandatory tags, such as title, keywords, descriptions, and author, are standard HTML tags that conscious and proficient Web-developers have been implementing for years. Beyond these general meta-tags, the NBII Program has implemented specific NBII meta-tags.

Currently, if a user accesses one of the search engines on the World Wide Web and searches for "common loon," the search result produces a hit list of more than 13 million results. Most of these results are likely pertinent to the user's query, but most are not relevant to the information need, and it is infeasible for a user to navigate through 13 million Web pages for relevant data.

Because of the NBII'S implementation of a refined and improved spidering methodology, users now can narrow their results lists to 62,000 Web pages. These spidered and indexed pages are primarily biological in nature due to the intellectual effort that is currently ongoing within the NBII Program for adding information content to the NBII System.

Users can further narrow their search results to 1,400 Web pages and information sources through the direct querying of meta-information contained within the "Common Name" meta-tag (Table 1). As one can imagine, this saves users tremendous time and presents authoritative and related information.

Some of the meta-tags described may or may not be appropriate for all NBII partner Web sites. We strongly encourage NBII partner sites offering specific species information to utilize our optional "Species Scientific Name" and "Species Common Name" tags for all relevant pages.

Because of the value of meta-tags to current search engine retrieval, as well as the promise of increased utilization by future search tools, the NBII is developing expanded meta-tagging guidelines and capabilities based upon the Dublin Core standard for documentation of electronic resources.

Two NBII partners, the U.S. Geological Survey's Patuxent Wildlife Research Center, and their Northern Prairie Wildlife Research Center, have realized immediate and lasting benefits from the implementation of current NBII recommendations for meta-tags. Using the Tag-Gen meta-tag generator customized for the NBII by Hiawatha Island Software, these science centers accomplished full meta-tag implementation across their entire sites in a matter of hours. Their data and information is now readily located and highly visible through a number of prominent search engines.

NBII PORTAL EFFORTS

Due to the multiple audiences NBII serves, and the varying level and scope of their biological information needs, the NBII recognized the key need to identify a paradigm for the delivery of this information to its partners, customers, and stakeholders.

To meet this need, the NBII is undertaking a pilot Web portal project. A portal is a single point of access to all agency or company data and information. The NBII Knowledge portal, http://my.nbii.gov, is designed to allow the various NBII users–including researchers, educators, natural resource mangers, and the general public–to identify what information content they are interested

TABLE 1. NBII Meta-Tags

Meta-Tag	Definition	Meta-Tag Format & Sample Value
Species Scientific Name	The Scientific Name of a particular Species on the web page being classified. NBII Partners are strongly encouraged to utilize the Integrated Taxonomic Information System (http://www.itis.usda.gov/plantproj/itis/index.html) as its basis for completing this information.	<meta name="Species Scientific Name" content="Parnassius smintheus">
Species Common Name	The Common Name of a particular Species on the web page being classified. The Common Name is extremely important to both expert and novice users when finding information about a particular species. The ITIS system is a source for completing this meta tag.	<meta name="Species Common Name" content="Rocky Mountain Parnassian">
Organization	The Organization who owns and maintains the specific web site and/or web page being classified. The use of standard controlled lists is strongly encouraged for completing this field.	<meta name="Organization" content="USGS Center for Biological Informatics">
NBII Theme	The High-level NBII Theme (Education, etc.) that your web page falls under. A list of values for this particular meta-tag can be found on the NBII web site.	<meta name="NBII Theme" content="Education">
NBII Category	The specific NBII Category, within the NBII Theme, that your web page falls under. A list of values for this particular meta-tag can be found on the NBII web site.	<meta name="NBII Category" content="General Curriculum">

in, and then present that content in a way that makes sense to users. The portal also acts as a virtual desktop, enabling biological information seekers to perform such necessary day-to-day tasks as accessing electronic mail, calendaring, travel logistics, and viewing newsfeeds and other Web content, within the portal itself.

The overall portal goals are:

- To provide each individual with customized "My Pages" that they personalize by selecting the applications, services, documents and data that are relevant to the functions that they perform each business day.
- To integrate existing NBII and USGS applications and content into a common delivery platform, and to make them accessible to a much larger audience, thus saving the user time during the discovery process.

- To notify proactively, or alert, users about critical situations or events, or the availability of new information through both the portal and e-mail, therefore enabling end users to react more quickly and make more informed natural resource or biodiversity-related decisions.
- To establish inter-node collaboration within the NBII enterprise and the community it serves. The portal will be the primary means of communication for all of the NBII Nodes. These Nodes are working on various biological and informatics issues across the United States. Currently, this group includes at least 150 federal, state, university, commercial, and non-profit organizations.
- To increase worker productivity by bringing together e-mail, calendaring, chat/messaging, and community forums all in one place.
- To provide a secure and manageable forum for "knowledge workers" to publish and subscribe to documents, reports, and data, and to increase the sharing of information between the NBII and partner organizations.
- To securely control access to the information from hundreds of enterprise sources without re-creating the existing security architecture, thereby reducing the time-to-delivery of the portal pilot and associated maintenance overhead.
- To provide access to other federally produced biological information resources through a single point of access. For example, as part of the pilot project, the NBII will also provide access to Department of Defense and National Institutes of Health biological information, including species distribution and habitat, and land resources. This will allow a user to access biological information produced and maintained by several federal agencies without having to know what federal agency is responsible for a particular resource or regional area.

The sample NBII Knowledge Portal shown in Figure 5 provides a representation of one of the "communities" within the portal. A portal community is a virtual location whereby project team members can interact in development of project goals, objectives, and deliverables. Communities are just one of the capabilities within the NBII Knowledge portal.

The NBII Knowledge Portal is continually evolving and capabilities are being added daily. As the various groups within the biological community begin to fully utilize the NBII Knowledge Portal, the portal's content and capabilities will expand, providing a single-point of access for all biological information on the Internet.

FIGURE 5. NBII Knowledge Portal

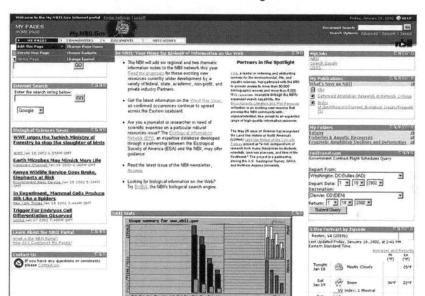

CSA PARTNERSHIP

The National Biological Information Infrastructure established a public/private partnership with CSA, a privately owned information company that has published abstracts and indexes to scientific research literature for more than thirty years, to provide access to "biocomplexity" information via the NBII site. Biocomplexity is commonly defined as the complex interaction of the Earth and its environment with people, plants, animals, and microbes (Raven 1994).

The partnership addresses a critical need within the information and scientific communities for a *single* dissemination point for biocomplexity information. This information is needed in the scientific and research communities, and by government agencies and the general public, to enable sound decision-making, identify new areas of research, and fully understand the relationships between people and their environment.

This unusual government/private sector partnership has made available, at no cost to users, more than 50,000 *proprietary* biocomplexity bibliographic citations. Furthermore, over 5,000 Web resources are also contained within the collection. A wide audience of users can thus enjoy unprecedented access to resources previously available only through subscription to indexing and abstracting service providers. XML DTDs and style sheets were developed to display the information, ensuring access both through the NBII search engine, and external ones. The NBII CSA collection of Citations and Web Resources is available through the NBII Search engine at: http://search.nbii.gov:9999/nbii/search.html.

CONCLUSION

As the World Wide Web continues to attract new users and grow exponentially in data, the importance of finding relevant, authoritative, biological information quickly and accurately becomes imperative. The NBII is the Nation's biological portal to all biological data and information within the United States, and is the U.S. contribution to several international initiatives; thus, it must continue to identify new and more effective means for the discovery, retrieval, and dissemination of these critical resources. Currently, one of the more effective methods for doing this is through the use of meta-information, the BioBot intelligent agent, the NBII Knowledge Portal, and the establishment of various public/private partnerships. As technology changes, so too will our approaches to solving this ever-growing and ongoing challenge.

REFERENCES

Fornwall, M. 2003. "Planning for OBIS: Examining Relationships with Existing National and International Biodiversity Information Systems." [In Prepress].

National Research Council. 1993. *A Biological Survey for the Nation*. Washington, DC: National Academy Press.

President's Committee of Advisors on Science and Technology Panel on Biodiversity and Ecosystems. 1998. *Teaming with Life: Investing in Science to Understand and Use America's Living Capital*. Executive Office of the President of the United States, 1998.

Raven, Peter. 1994. "Defining Biodiversity." *Nature Conservancy*, Jan./Feb., 11.

Syracuse Research Corporation's Chemical Information Databases: Extraction and Compilation of Data Related to Environmental Fate and Exposure

Sarah A. Rosenberg
Amy E. Hueber
Dallas Aronson
Sybil Gouchie
Philip H. Howard
William M. Meylan
Jay L. Tunkel

SUMMARY. Some types of data useful in the study and assessment of a chemical's environmental fate and toxicity are physical and chemical properties, degradation tests, monitoring data, field studies, toxicology and carcinogenesis studies, and regulatory information. Syracuse Research Corporation produces and maintains several databases relating to this field, including the Environmental Fate Database (EFDB), PHYSPROP (physical properties database), TSCATS (test submissions under the Toxic Substances and Control Act), SOLVDB (solvents database), SMILECAS

Sarah A. Rosenberg, Amy E. Hueber, Dallas Aronson, Sybil Gouchie, Philip H. Howard, William M. Meylan, and Jay L. Tunkel are all affiliated with the Syracuse Research Corporation, Syracuse, NY 13212.

Address correspondence to: Amy E. Hueber (E-mail: hueber@syrres.com).

[Haworth co-indexing entry note]: "Syracuse Research Corporation's Chemical Information Databases: Extraction and Compilation of Data Related to Environmental Fate and Exposure." Rosenberg, Sarah A. et al. Co-published simultaneously in *Science & Technology Libraries* (The Haworth Information Press, an imprint of The Haworth Press, Inc.) Vol. 23, No. 4, 2003, pp. 73-87; and: *Online Ecological and Environmental Data* (ed: Virginia Baldwin) The Haworth Information Press, an imprint of The Haworth Press, Inc., 2003, pp. 73-87. Single or multiple copies of this article are available for a fee from The Haworth Document Delivery Service [1-800-HAWORTH, 9:00 a.m. - 5:00 p.m. (EST). E-mail address: docdelivery@haworthpress.com].

Digital Object Identifier: 10.1300/J122v23n04_06

(Simplified Molecular Input Line Entry System notations database), Chemical Pointers (pointers to databases and regulatory lists), and Global Warming Potentials. This article describes the structure, content, characteristics and development of the databases. *[Article copies available for a fee from The Haworth Document Delivery Service: 1-800-HAWORTH. E-mail address: <docdelivery@ haworthpress.com> Website: <http://www.HaworthPress.com> © 2003 by The Haworth Press, Inc. All rights reserved.]*

KEYWORDS. Environmental chemistry, environmental fate, toxicology, environmental health, database, chemical data

INTRODUCTION

With the current proliferation of information on the Internet, one thing is clear: the importance of well-organized sources of plentiful, reliable data. An area in which good resources are needed, and which is a subject of concern for many researchers, government agencies, members of business and industry, and the public, is the study and assessment of how chemicals can impact health and the environment.

Assessment of a chemical's impact includes consideration of both its toxicity (to people and other organisms), and its behavior when it enters the environment, or environmental fate (Howard et al. 1978). The extent and nature of human or wildlife exposure to a chemical depend on how long the chemical persists in the environment, and which environmental media it reaches. These two factors are determined by the extent and nature of the chemical's tendency to transform or degrade, via chemical, photochemical, or microbial means, as well as its ability to be transported within and between water, soil and air. Types of information relevant to assessing toxicity include, but are not limited to, acute and chronic effects studies via applicable routes of exposure, carcinogenicity studies, and studies on reproductive and developmental toxicity. Data important to the study of environmental fate include transport and degradation tests, monitoring data, and field studies, as well as chemical and physical properties (Howard et al. 1987). The field of estimation and modeling, which seeks to predict environmental behavior of chemicals, also requires data sets to use in development and evaluation.

The Environmental Science Center (ESC) division of Syracuse Research Corporation (SRC) has been creating and maintaining information products related to environmental fate and toxicology since the late 1970s. Databases developed at SRC include the Environmental Fate Database (EFDB), a set of files providing quick access to the available fate data on a given chemical;

PHYSPROP, a database of chemical structures, names and physical properties for over 25,000 chemicals; and TSCATS, a database which provides subject indexing of unpublished industry studies submitted to the United States Environmental Protection Agency (EPA) under the Toxic Substances Control Act. The usefulness of each database is due to the process of applying scientific expertise in identifying pertinent data, and extracting, compiling, indexing, and making the information searchable and accessible. Examples of this process, particularly EFDB, and also the databases PHYSPROP, TSCATS, SOLVDB, SMILECAS, Chem Pointer, and Global Warming Potentials are discussed in this article. Information about other software, products and services can be found on the ESC Website at http://esc.syrres.com.

DATABASES

Environmental Fate Database (EFDB)
http://esc.syrres.com/interkow/database.htm

The Environmental Fate Database, developed with the sponsorship of the Environmental Protection Agency, is primarily composed of four separate databases: DATALOG, CHEMFATE, BIOLOG, and BIODEG. DATALOG and BIOLOG provide bibliographic citations to fate-related studies. Each article is thoroughly indexed not only by chemical, but also by categories of data that are discussed. (See sections on DATALOG and BIOLOG in this article for examples of data categories used.) CHEMFATE and BIODEG are data files, much more time-consuming to produce, since each article is analyzed, data extracted, and values are entered in appropriate fields. All files are interrelated via a file of Chemical Abstracts Service (CAS) Registry Numbers (unique numerical identifiers) containing over 20,000 chemicals with preferred name and formula; and by a bibliographic file called XREF, containing full references for articles cited. The intended users of EFDB are environmental researchers, chemical manufacturers, environmental consultants, and those in academic research in the field of environmental chemistry.

Data Collection

EFDB began in the late 1970s with a project to collect data on a test set of 200 chemicals chosen in cooperation with EPA from a list of 600 chemicals whose annual production was greater than one million pounds (Howard et al. 1981). Online bibliographic databases were searched, including *Chemical Abstracts*, *NTIS (National Technical Information Service)*, *SciSearch*, *Pollution Abstracts*, *Oceanic*

Abstracts, *Enviroline*, *APTIC (Air Pollution Technical Information Control)*, *Environmental Bibliography*, *Agricola*, and *Aquatic Science and Fisheries Abstracts*. Data types to include in the *Environmental Fate Database* were chosen, and data was then added to DATALOG and CHEMFATE.

From those relatively small beginnings, the database has developed and expanded greatly in the ensuing decades, with new material constantly being added. Data retrieval proceeds in a number of ways. Relevant literature is identified in the course of activities of Environmental Science Center scientists. Online searching is performed in a variety of databases relevant to particular research topics, though *Chemical Abstracts* has always been the most important database for finding environmental fate-related citations. Current awareness publications such as *Current Contents*, as well as a core set of journals, are scanned for relevant material on a frequent basis. Review articles are another excellent source for information on specific research publications. Citations are screened and selected by senior researchers and the articles are obtained through a variety of means, including in-house journal subscriptions, requests to authors for reprints, interlibrary loan, and document delivery services.

Articles are read and analyzed by trained staff. Descriptive information and data are entered into the EFDB catalog system using PC-based PARADOX software, a vast improvement in both efficiency and accuracy from the key punch card system originally employed. These files are electronically transferred to a VAX mainframe and added to the main files. Electronic cataloging alerts the cataloger to duplicate entries, greatly expedites data entry, and allows for spell checking of citation entries. This insures prompt availability of information to the technical writing staff.

DATALOG

The DATALOG file currently contains 367,000 records on 16,000 chemicals, organized by CAS number and cataloged under any of 18 data types, listed in Table 1. A sample output is given in Figure 1.

BIOLOG

With the realization that microbes may play an important role in chemical spill remediation, BIOLOG was developed to further subdivide biodegradation data into specific categories, enabling the user to quickly identify relevant studies. The file contains 68,000 records on 8,000 chemicals. Indexing Codes are listed in Table 2, with a sample output illustrated in Figure 2.

TABLE 1. DATALOG Categories

ADSORP - Adsorption	HENRY CON - Henry's Law constant
BIOCON - Bioconcentration	HYDROL - Hydrolysis
BIODEG - Biodegradation	MONIT - Monitoring - Air, Water, and Soil
DISS CON - Dissociation Constant	OCCUP - Occupational Concentrations
ECOS - Ecosystem	O/W PART - Octanol/Water Partition Coefficient
EFFL - Effluent Concentrations	PHOTOOXID - Photoxidation
EVAW - Evaporation from Water	UV - UV Spectra
FIELD - Field Studies	VP - Vapor pressure
FOOD - Food and Crop Concentrations	WSOL - Water Solubility

FIGURE 1. Sample DATALOG Output

```
ADSORP     MEREDITH, CE & RADOSEVICH, M (1998)        ( 290)
EVAP       GHERINI, SA ET AL. (1989)         ( 194)
FIELD      BROHOLM, K ET AL. (2000)          ( 336)
HYDROL     CHOUDHRY, GG (1983A)              (  42)
OCCUP      THRANE,KE & STRAY,H (1986)          ( 101)
O/W PART   BORISOVER,MD & GRABER,ER (1997)         ( 280)
PHOTOOXID  ATKINSON,R ET AL. (1995B)           ( 248)
UV         FEILBERG,A ET AL. (1996)          ( 266)
VP         NENDZA,M & HERMENS,J (1995)          ( 322)
WATER SOL   YALKOWSKY,SH & DANNENFELSER,RM (1992)     ( 216)
```

27341 ATKINSON,R.; TUAZON,E.C.; AREY,J.; ASCHMANN,S.M.; 1995B*
  ATMOSPHERIC AND INDOOR CHEMISTRY OF GAS-PHASE INDOLE, QUINOLINE, AND
  ISOQUINOLINE.
  ATMOS. ENVIRON.
  29:3423-32

31670 BORISOVER,M.D.; GRABER,E.R.; 1997 *
  SPECIFIC INTERACTIONS OF ORGANIC COMPOUNDS WITH SOIL ORGANIC CARBON.
  CHEMOSPHERE
  34:1761-76

[continued...]

CHEMFATE

CHEMFATE is a data value file reporting summaries, results, and experimental conditions and contains information in 17,200 records on 1,728 chemicals. The annotated entries indicate whether results were calculated, values refereed, units converted, etc. Data categories are listed in Table 3 with a sample output given in Figure 3.

TABLE 2. BIOLOG Indexing Codes

B - Biodegradation	AE - Aerobic	MC - Mixed Culture	SEW - Sewage	R- Reaction Pathway	D - DATALOG
T - Toxicity	AN - Aerobic	PC - Pure Culture	SOI - Soil		H - Hydrocarbons
		CF - Cell Free Extract	SED - Sediment		A - Aromatics
		PE - Pure Enzyme	WAF - Fresh Water		M - Metals
			WAM - Marine Water		P - Pesticides
			OTH - Other		G - General

FIGURE 2. Sample BIOLOG Output

CAS #: 000091-22-5   Name: QUINOLINE

```
B AN MC  SOI  D  ARVIN,E ET AL. (1989A)
B AN MC WAF  D  ARVIN,E ET AL. (1989A)
B AN MC SED  D  BAK,F & WIDDEL,F (1986A)
B AN MC SED  D  CATALLO,WJ (1996)
B AE  PC  SOI  D  CHAMBERS,CW & KABLER,PW (1964)
B AE  PC  SOI  D  OLOUGHLIN,EJ ET AL. (1999)
B AE  PC  SOI  D  PANDEY,RA & SANDHYA,S (1991)
```

ARVIN,E ET AL. (1989A)
ARVIN,E.; JENSEN,B.; GODSY,E.M.; GRBIC-GALIC,D.; MICROBIAL DEGRADATION
OF OIL AND CREOSOTE RELATED AROMATIC COMPOUNDS UNDER AEROBIC AND
ANAEROBIC CONDITIONS.; INT. CONF. PHYSIOCHEMICAL BIOL. DETOXIF. HAZARD.
WASTES; 2:828-47; 1989A

BAK,F & WIDDEL,F (1986A)
BAK,F.; WIDDEL,F.; ANAEROBIC DEGRADATION OF INDOLIC COMPOUNDS BY
SULFATE-REDUCING ENRICHMENT CULTURES, AND DESCRIPTION OF
DESULFOBACTERIUM INDOLICUM GEN. NOV., SP. NOV.; ARCH. MICROBIOL.;
146:170-6; 1986A

[continued...]

BIODEG

BIODEG is likewise a data value file containing over 5,800 records on 800 chemicals. The 800 chemicals indexed in the BIODEG database represent a broad sampling of commercial chemicals with both available biodegradation data and diverse chemical structures so that the database can be used for development of quantitative structure biodegradation relationships (QSBRs). The

TABLE 3. CHEMFATE Data Categories

ID - Identification	SCOL - Soil column transport
MF - Molecular Formula	SRF - Soil thin-layer chromatography
MW - Molecular Weight	**LDEG - Laboratory Degradation**
PNAME - Preferred name	ECOS - Ecosystem
SYN - Synonym	HYDR - Hydrolysis
CP - Chemical Property	MICD - Microbial degradation
LOGP - log Octanol/water partition coefficient	NYSD - Degradation in natural systems
PKA - log Acid dissociation constant	OXID - Oxidation and other reactions
SOIA - Soil adsorption constant	PHOT - Photolysis
UV - Ultraviolet adsorption	**EM - Environmental Measurement**
VP - Vapor pressure	AIRM - Air monitoring
WSOL - Water solubility	BIOM - Biota monitoring
TRAN - Transport Properties	FIEL - Field studies
BIOC - log Bioconcentration factor	SOIM - Soil monitoring
EVAW - Evaporation from water - T 1/2	WATM - Water Monitoring
HENL - Henry's Law constant	

organization of biodegradation test data is in four areas: screening tests, biological treatment simulation tests, grab sample tests, and field studies (Howard et al. 1986). An overall summary code (Figure 4) is assigned to each chemical describing the compounds' susceptibility to microbial degradation. Figure 5 illustrates a sample BIODEG record.

XREF

All of these databases are supported by the full reference citation database, XREF, which contains 35,200 records, using the format presented in Figure 6.

Access

The databases that comprise EFDB are now completely accessible to the public from the company website under the partial sponsorship of the U.S. Environmental Protection Agency and some other industry supporters. Enhanced search capabilities, such as batch searching, are available in the licensed commercial Windows versions.

Originally, these files were designed to meet the needs of in-house research through ready-access to topical literature citations, enabling quick turn-around time following information requests. The databases were after-

FIGURE 3. Sample CHEMFATE Output

CAS #: 000091_22_5   Name: QUINOLINE

```
*************************************************************************
ID    QUINOLINE                         CAS#   91_22_5
  Preferred Name :  QUINOLINE
  9th Col Index  :  QUINOLINE
  Synonym        :  1_AZANAPHTHALENE
  Mol. Weight    :  129.17
  Mol. Formula   :  C9H7N
*************************************************************************


PKA   QUINOLINE                         CAS#   91_22_5
  Dissoc Constant: 4.90
  Temperature (C): 20
  Remarks        : SRC RECOMMENDED VALUE
  Abbrev. Ref.   : WEAST,RC ET AL. (1985)
*************************************************************************


LOGP  QUINOLINE                         CAS#   91_22_5
  Log O/W Part.  : 2.03
  Remarks        : RECOMMENDED VALUE
  Abbrev. Ref.   : HANSCH,C & LEO,AJ (1985)
*************************************************************************


VP    QUINOLINE                         CAS#   91_22_5
  Vapor Pressure : 6.000E_02  MM HG    MEASURED
  Temperature (C): 25
  Remarks        : SRC RECOMMENDED VALUE
  Abbrev. Ref.   : DAUBERT,TE & DANNER,RP (1989)
*************************************************************************


PHOT  QUINOLINE                         CAS#   91_22_5
  Summary      : PHOTOLYSIS IN WATER
  System       : SOLVENT
  Rate         : 7.7E_7    1/SEC
  Half Life    : 250 (HR)
  Quantum Yield : 3.3E_4
  Wavelength (NM): 313 (NM)
  Remarks      : RATE CONSTANT AND HALF_LIFE CALCULATED FOR LATE JUNE AT
                 40  DEG N LATITUDE
  Abbrev. Ref.  : MILL,T ET AL. (1981)
*************************************************************************
```

ward made available via dial-up access to outside corporations for a fee. This was followed by the generation of zipped interactive files which could be unzipped directly to the users desktops, allowing marketing to overseas users who were previously unable to access the data due to prohibitive dial-up costs or incompatible modem software. The advent of the Internet has since provided the medium for easy public access.

FIGURE 4. BIODEG Study Evaluation Codes

BFA - Biodegrades Fast with Acclimation
BF - Biodegrades Fast
BSA - Biodegrades Slow with Acclimation
BS - Biodegrades Slow
BST - Biodegrades Sometimes
NB - No Biodegradation

FIGURE 5. Sample BIODEG Search Result

```
******************************************************************************
CAS #:   91-22-5   QUINOLINE
Parameter Type   : Screening Test
Study Biodeg Eval:  BS
Rate             : 0-29
Units            : %BODT
Test Method      : JAPANESE MITI
Oxygen Condition : AEROBIC
Analysis Method  : BOD
Incub Time (days): 14
Chem Conc (ppm)  : 100
Microbial Pop    : 30 (MG/L)
Inoculum         : ACTIVATED SLUDGE
Temp (deg C)     : 25
pH               : 7.0
Reference        : SASAKI,S (1978)
******************************************************************************
```

Physical Properties Database (PHYSPROP)
http://esc.syrres.com/interkow/database.htm

The PHYSPROP database provides the user with a chemical structure and environmentally relevant physical/chemical properties, with information being obtained from the open literature as well as the DATALOG and CHEMFATE files. Data include melting point, boiling point, water solubility, octanol/water partition coefficient, vapor pressure, dissociation constant, the Henry's Law constant, and hydroxyl radical reaction rate constant. On the Web, single chemicals can be searched via CAS Registry number. Additional features, such as substructure searching, are available with the desktop versions. This and other SRC databases can now also be simultaneously substructure searched on the website (see Chemical Pointer section for details). The data are supported with the reference citations from XREF (Figure 7 gives a sample output). PHYSPROP contains over 25,000 chemicals. More chemicals and values are periodically added to PHYSPROP as data are identified.

FIGURE 6. Sample XREF Records

BROHOLM,K ET AL. (2000)
BROHOLM,K.; NILSSON,B.; SIDLE,R.C.; ARVIN,E.; TRANSPORT AND
BIODEGRADATION OF CREOSOTE COMPOUNDS IN CLAYEY TILL, A FIELD
EXPERIMENT.; J. CONTAM. HYDROL.; 41:239-60; 2000

LOPES,TJ & FURLONG,ET (2001)
LOPES,T.J.; FURLONG,E.T.; OCCURRENCE AND POTENTIAL ADVERSE EFFECTS OF
SEMIVOLATILE ORGANIC COMPOUNDS IN STREAMBED SEDIMENT, UNITED STATES,
1992-1995.; ENVIRON. SCI. TECHNOL.; 20:727-37; 2001

FIGURE 7. Sample PHYSPROP Output

CAS #: 000091-22-5				QUINOLINE
Formula: C_9H_7N				
Mol Weight: 129.16				
MP (deg C): -14.78		FP (deg C):		
BP (deg C): 237.1				
BP pressure (mm Hg):				

Property/Value	Units	Temp	Data Type	Reference
Wsol 6.11E+003	mg/L	25	EXP	SMITH,JH ET AL. (1978)
logP 2.03			EXP	HANSCH,C ET AL. (1995)
VP 6.00E-002	mm Hg	25	EXP	DAUBERT,TE & DANNER,RP (1989)
DC 4.90	pKa	20	EXP	WEAST,RC ET AL. (1985)
HL 1.67E-006	atm m3/mol	25	EST	VP/WSOL
OH 1.16E-011	cm3/molc sec	24	EXP	ATKINSON,R ET AL. (1995B)

Toxic Substances Control Act Test Submissions Database (TSCATS)
http://esc.syrres.com/interkow/database.htm

The Toxic Substances Control Act (TSCA), enacted by Congress in 1976, gives the Environmental Protection Agency the ability to identify and control new and existing industrial chemicals produced in or imported into the United States. TSCA requires that new chemicals be tested and reviewed for risks to health and the environment before they can be manufactured; industry must submit any available pertinent studies. The TSCATS database, developed in cooperation with the EPA in 1985, provides a system for organizing, storing, and providing access to these unpublished reports submitted under the Act (Santodonato et al. 1987).

In addition to entering details of the submissions (submitting organization, CAS number, and date of test, for example) to the database, SRC staff categorize the reports as involving health effects, environmental effects, or environmental fate. Within these subject categories, a hierarchy of controlled terms allows more in-depth indexing, so as to indicate the purposes of a study (for example carcinogenicity), species tested, and elements of the experimental design (e.g., route of administration, or whether the chemical was used by itself or within a mixture). In addition, abstracts are created for many of the studies. Thus, database records identify the reports, which are filed and stored in microfiche format, via a fiche number, and provide key information about report content. The TSCATS version available on the SRC Website can be searched by CAS#, study type, or an index of chemical names or formulas can be used, and the search can be limited by study type, organism, or route of administration. Figure 8 shows an example of TSCATS output.

SMILECAS Database
http://esc.syrres.com/interkow/database.htm

SMILES is an acronym for Simplified Molecular Input Line Entry System, which is a chemical notation system used to represent a molecular structure by a linear string of symbols. SMILECAS is a modified SMILES developed by SRC for use by the SRC programs, the slight difference involving entry and detection of aromaticity. The database contains notations for over 103,000 chemicals, allowing users to enter a CAS number and thus have the SMILES notation (Figure 9) and structure automatically entered into software called EPIWIN, which was developed for estimating physical, chemical and fate properties from structures, and is available for free from the U.S. EPA Website at http://www.epa.gov/oppt/p2framework/docs/epiwin.htm.

Solvents Database (SOLVDB)
http://solvdb.ncms.org/

SRC developed SOLVDB for the National Center for Manufacturing Sciences as a way to compare various properties of solvents. This was in response to the phasing out of chlorofluorocarbon (CFC) solvents. The database is now available through NCMS at the URL address http://solvdb.ncms.org/.

The information contained in SOLVDB can be accessed in a number of ways. Starting with a specific solvent, you can obtain a variety of information about the solvent, including synonyms, chemical and physical data, possible suppliers, potential substitutes for the solvent, and health and safety informa-

FIGURE 8. Sample TSCATS Output

CAS #: 000091-22-5   Name: QUINOLINE

CAS #	Name	Study	Purpose	Organism	Rte	Admin	Test	Ref
91-22-5	QUINOLINE	HE	DIRR	MAMM	RABB	DERM	SNGL	1
91-22-5	QUINOLINE	HE	EPID					2
91-22-5	QUINOLINE	HE	EPID					3
91-22-5	QUINOLINE	HE	EPID					4
91-22-5	QUINOLINE	HE	EPID					5
91-22-5	QUINOLINE	HE	EPID					6
91-22-5	QUINOLINE	HE	EPID	MAMM	HUMN			7
91-22-5	QUINOLINE	HE	EPID	MAMM	HUMN			8
91-22-5	QUINOLINE	HE	EPID	MAMM	HUMN			9
91-22-5	QUINOLINE	HE	EPID	MAMM	HUMN			10

[continued.........]

** Number of studies =   40
** Number of references =   26

1- 400180 4 HOUR DOT CORROSIVE TEST ON RABBITS
    U.S. EPA/OPTS Public Files
    Fiche #: OTS0516151
    Doc#: 86-870001570   Old#:   Sect: 8D
    Produced: 09/25/74
    Received: 08/12/87 MELLON INSTI
    Chem: NAPHTHALENE (91-20-3)

2- 31278 MORTALITY AMONG KOPPERS WORKERS EMPLOYED AT EIGHT COAL TAR
    FACILITIES WITH COVER LETTER DATED 012585
    U.S. EPA/OPTS Public Files
    Fiche #: OTS0000385-0   Loc: 1;1 - 2;1 (12)
    Doc#: FYI-OTS-0285-0385   Old#:   Sect: FYI
    Produced: 02/25/82 TABERSHAW OCC MEDICINE ASSOC
    Received: 02/25/85 KOPPERS CO INC
    Chem: COAL TAR CHEMICALS

3- 31283 CROSS-SECTIONAL HEALTH STUDY OF WORKERS AT THE FOLLANSBEE, WEST
    VIRGINIA PLANT OF KOPPERS COMPANY, INC
    U.S. EPA/OPTS Public Files
    Fiche #: OTS0000385-0   Loc: 4;5 - 5;3 (12)
    Doc#: FYI-OTS-0285-0385   Old#:   Sect: FYI
    Produced: 08/14/79 TABERSHAW OCC MEDICINE ASSOC
    Received: 02/25/85 KOPPERS CO INC
    Chem: COAL TAR CHEMICALS

4- 31284 CROSS-SECTIONAL HEALTH STUDY OF WORKERS AT NINE KOPPERS COAL TAR
    PLANTS COMBINED REPORT
    U.S. EPA/OPTS Public Files
    Fiche #: OTS0000385-0   Loc: 2;6 - 3;4 (12)
    Doc#: FYI-OTS-0285-0385   Old#:   Sect: FYI
    Produced: 05/01/81 TABERSHAW OCC MEDICINE ASSOC
    Received: 02/25/85 KOPPERS CO INC
    Chem: COAL TAR CHEMICALS

5- 31289 CROSS-SECTIONAL HEALTH STUDY OF WORKERS AT THE CHICAGO, ILLINOIS
    PLANT OF KOPPERS COMPANY
    U.S. EPA/OPTS Public Files
    Fiche #: OTS0000385-0   Loc: 3;5 - 4;4 (12)
    Doc#: FYI-OTS-0285-0385   Old#:   Sect: FYI
    Produced: 07/25/80 TABERSHAW OCC MEDICINE ASSOC
    Received: 02/25/85 KOPPERS CO INC
    Chem: COAL TAR CHEMICALS

6-[continued........]

tion. It is also searchable by a set of criteria pertinent to a particular application and will list all solvents in the database falling into a range of desired solvent properties, all solvents in the database not falling into specific toxicity, regulatory, or environmental categories, or all solvents in the database falling into specific chemical categories. This facilitates identification of alternative solvents that may be used.

Global Warming Potentials (GWP) / Ozone Depletion Potentials (ODP)
http://esc.syrres.com/ozone.asp

This file contains global warming potentials and ozone depletion potentials, ratios that describe a chemical's potential to contribute to the greenhouse effect or to impact the ozone layer. In the 1990s, SRC developed a simple methodology for a qualitative determination of a chemical's GWP (Tunkel et al. 1986). However, the values here are quantitative, experimental values, compiled from the open literature. The database is updated irregularly, and there are currently 186 records. Figure 10 provides a sample record.

Chemical Pointer File
http://esc.syrres.com/interkow/database.htm

The Chemical Pointer File contains records for approximately 22,000 chemicals, and provides pointers to information in different databases. The chemicals included are those from several of SRC's databases, consisting mainly of discrete organic compounds from the TSCA Inventory, chlorofluorocarbons and chlorofluorocarbon substitutes, pesticides, and biologically active compounds. Chemical Pointer is currently available as an ISISBase database.

FIGURE 9. SMILES Notation for Guinoline (C9H7N)

Quinoline - n(c(c(ccc1)cc2)c1)c2

FIGURE 10. Sample GWP/ODP Output for 1,1,1-Trichloroethane

CAS Number:		000071-55-6
Chemical Name:	Ethane, 1,1,1-trichloro-	
GWP:		360(20), 110(100), 35(500) *CO2
ODP:		0.15
GWP Ref:	Albritton, DL, et al (1994)	
ODP Ref:	Ravishankara AR & Lovejoy ER (1994)	

CO2 is the Reference compound. Time horizon relative to CO2 is indicated in parenthesis.

For each chemical, the ISISBase file provides name, structure, and CAS number, and indicates which of the covered databases and regulatory lists include the chemical. Pointers include: EPA's List of Lists, Superfund Amendments and Reauthorization Act (SARA) Section 313 Toxic Release Inventory (TRI) chemicals, SARA Section 302 Extremely Hazardous chemicals, Comprehensive Environmental Response, Compensation, and Liability Act (CERCLA) Reportable Quantity chemicals, Resource Conservation and Recovery Act (RCRA) Reportable Quantity chemicals, Toxic Substances Control Act (TSCA) Inventory, National Library of Medicine's Hazardous Substances Data Bank (HSDB), the individual files of SRC's EFDB, the proprietary SRC database FATE/EXPOS, the Pomona College MEDCHEM data base of octanol/water partition coefficients, and the ARIZONA dATABASE of water solubility values from Samuel Yalkowsky at the University of Arizona.

Structure search capability is a useful feature of the database. Both exact structure searching and substructure searching are available. A major benefit of the substructure search capability is that for a compound of interest, other compounds with similar functional groups can be identified, and data on each can be more quickly located and compared.

The Chemical Pointer File has also begun to be used as a basis for performing time-saving structure and substructure searches of PHYSPROP, TSCATS, and the files of EFDB, all at once. On the Environmental Science Center Website, proprietary Web-based chemical structure query software developed by SRC, called ChemS[3], now provides an easy-to-use interface (see http://esc.syrres.com/). When the pointer database is searched via ChemS[3], all matching chemical structures are shown. Beside each chemical is displayed a list of links to SRC databases that have data for that chemical. Fom this search result screen, chemical and physical properties from the PHYSPROP database can be displayed with one click. The free Web-based Chemical Pointer file therefore provides a central access point, with substructure search capability, to several of SRC's databases.

CONCLUSION

Databases created, developed and maintained at Syracuse Research Corporation's Environmental Science Center continue to provide enhanced access to data related to health and environmental impacts of chemicals. This includes environmental fate data, chemical and physical properties, health and environmental toxicology studies, and other information. The databases can assist researchers and other users, including those in academia, business and industry, and government, by decreasing the time, effort and cost of finding data.

REFERENCES

Howard P.H. and A.E. Hueber. 1987. Biodegradation data evaluation for structure/biodegradability relations. *Environmental Toxicology and Chemistry* 6, 1-10.

Howard, P.H., A. E. Hueber, B.C. Mulesky, J.S. Crisman, W. Meylan, E. Crosbie, D.A. Gray, G.W. Sage, K.P. Howard, and A. LaMacchia. 1986. BIOLOG, BIODEG, and FATE/EXPOS: New files on microbial degradation and toxicity as well as environmental fate/exposure of chemicals. *Environmental Toxicology and Chemistry* 5, 977-988.

Howard, P.H., G.W. Sage, A. LaMacchia, and A. Colb. 1981. The development of an Environmental Fate Data Base. *Journal of Chemical Information and Computer Sciences* 22, 38-44.

Howard, P.H., J. Saxena, and H. Sikka. 1978. Determining the fate of chemicals. *Environmental Science and Technology* 12, 398-407.

Santodonato, J., C. Bush, P. Howard, K. Howard, and S. DelFavero. 1987. TSCATS: A database for chemical and subject indexing of health and environmental studies submitted under the Toxic Substances Control Act. *Environmental Toxicology and Chemistry* 6, 921-927.

Tunkel, J.L., D. Aronson, H. Printup, and P.H. Howard. 1996. *Assessment of substitute chemicals and their potential global warming, ozone depletion, and human health effects. I. Semiconductor industry substitutes.* Prepared for the Atmospheric Pollution Prevention Division, Office of Atmospheric Programs, U.S. EPA, under Contract 68-D2-0182.

Convergence and Dissemination:
A Brief History and Description
of the StreamNet Project

Lenora A. Oftedahl

SUMMARY. The StreamNet Project has grown from the combination of two projects into a premier source for data on fish and fisheries in the Columbia Basin. As data is collected, it is added to the tables and trends on the StreamNet Internet site. The StreamNet Project website serves as a portal to this data and other independent data sets.

The StreamNet Library has grown as well, and provides full library services to the researchers and decisionmakers in the Columbia River Basin. One of the initiatives of the library is to digitize as much of the grey literature pertaining to the basin as possible. *[Article copies available for a fee from The Haworth Document Delivery Service: 1-800-HAWORTH. E-mail address: <docdelivery@haworthpress.com> Website: <http://www.HaworthPress.com> © 2003 by The Haworth Press, Inc. All rights reserved.]*

KEYWORDS. Salmon, Columbia River basin, data exchange, cooperation, digital archives, GIS, interactive maps

---

Lenora A. Oftedahl, MLS, is StreamNet Regional Librarian, Columbia River Inter-Tribal Fish Commission, 729 NE Oregon Street, Suite 190, Portland, OR 97232 (E-mail: OFTL@critfc.org).

[Haworth co-indexing entry note]: "Convergence and Dissemination: A Brief History and Description of the StreamNet Project." Oftedahl, Lenora A. Co-published simultaneously in *Science & Technology Libraries* (The Haworth Information Press, an imprint of The Haworth Press, Inc.) Vol. 23, No. 4, 2003, pp. 89-94; and: *Online Ecological and Environmental Data* (ed: Virginia Baldwin) The Haworth Information Press, an imprint of The Haworth Press, Inc., 2003, pp. 89-94. Single or multiple copies of this article are available for a fee from The Haworth Document Delivery Service [1-800-HAWORTH, 9:00 a.m. - 5:00 p.m. (EST). E-mail address: docdelivery@haworthpress.com].

89

INTRODUCTION AND BACKGROUND

Data sharing systems became popular in the early 1990s with the advent of the Internet and the World Wide Web. At this time there were two related projects in the Columbia River Basin to gather data on threatened and endangered salmon and their habitat. The Northwest Environmental Database (NED) gathered information on river reaches and aquatic habitat. The Coordinated Information System (CIS) gathered statistics and data about Pacific salmon in the Columbia River Basin, as well as documentation to reference the data. These documents were added to the existing library at the Columbia River Inter-Tribal Fish Commission (CRITFC).

Each of the predecessors, NED and CIS, contributed knowledge and information. In 1995 the Bonneville Power Administration merged the two projects "to create a consolidated, high quality package of data products and services to address emerging Fish and Wildlife Program data needs and to realize cost savings" (Steering Committee, 1996, 2). The StreamNet Project (Fish Data for the Northwest) was born. The StreamNet Project (http://www.streamnet.org) has always been an Internet project. The primary purpose was to deliver data directly to the researcher/scientist/decision maker/planner at their desktops so they would not have to spend precious time tracking down information. The requirement to provide documentation for all data entries was carried over from CIS to the StreamNet Project. As participating agencies provided documents, the StreamNet Library soon overshadowed the CRITFC library.

StreamNet PROJECT

The Statement of Work for the StreamNet Project outlines all of the data collection and dissemination services provided to the general public. The need for this project was outlined in one of the first project summaries submitted to the Bonneville Power Administration: "Virtually every analysis of the Pacific Northwest fish issue calls for preparation of regionally consistent and easily accessible data. StreamNet seeks to fulfill this need by providing essential baseline data on fish distribution, production, habitat, and management that is useful for regional policy, planning, management, and research activities" (Steering Committee, 1996, 3).

As a regional effort by state, federal and tribal agencies to exchange data on fish and habitat in the Pacific Northwest, the project created a data exchange format for each agency to use when submitting data. This helped solve the problem of previous efforts with data generation in a multitude of formats. Very often, the data was not in any standardized format and was lost in someone's filing cabinet. Participants in the project include Oregon Dept. of Fish and Wildlife, Washington Dept. of Fish and Wildlife, Idaho Dept. of Fish and Game, Montana Dept. of Fish, Wildlife and Parks, Shoshone-Bannock Tribes (withdrew in 2001), Columbia River Inter-Tribal Fish Commission and the U.S. Fish and Wildlife Service. The National Marine Fisheries Service, Environmental Protection Agency, U.S. Forest Service and Geological Survey are cooperators. Use of the interagency model allows cooperation between the states and federal agencies when species are being evaluated for Endangered or Threatened status under the Endangered Species Act. The collective process makes data collection more thorough and more easily defensible. The cooperating agencies and participants also gain insight into how other agencies are managed. This insight makes cooperation in other areas more likely.

Library

One of the most important standards for data development is that each data element is linked to a document. The StreamNet Library houses the reference documents for the online data. When a data trend is displayed, the last column in the tables lists a reference number for footnotes at the bottom of the screen (Figure 1). The footnotes list the complete citation for the reference. The user also has the ability to click on the title of the document and be taken to a library catalog entry for the document. Many of these documents are "grey" or even "black" literature; most are unpublished. There are some primary materials, including actual stream survey forms as well as more popular literature like *A Waterfall Lover's Guide to the Pacific Northwest*. The StreamNet Library provides the full-range of library services to its clients through the website http://www.fishlib.org. Most services are free, but the materials will only circulate as interlibrary loans to other libraries. In addition to the StreamNet Reference documents, the library collects materials on fisheries, aquatic sciences, conservation, forestry, ecology, hydrology, environmental sciences, Native American studies, and the history of the Columbia Basin.

Data

The online data sets of the StreamNet Project include anadromous fish production and survival (natural and hatchery), resident fish production and survival, wildlife, aquatic habitat including water quality, facilities such as dams and hatcheries, mitigation projects, and river operations. Both the anadromous and resident fish areas include species and life stage specific datasets. Each year the StreamNet Project steering committee meets to decide on data priorities. The steering committee additionally decides what new data should be col-

FIGURE 1. Sample of Results from a Data Query (Reference Citation at Lower Edge)

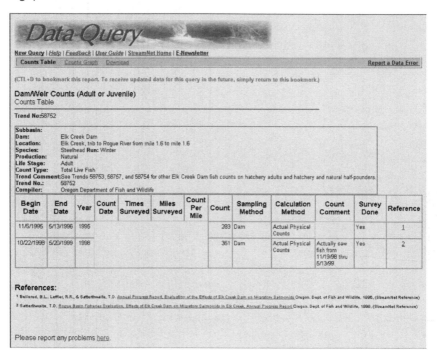

lected. These discussions are driven by user requests and the Northwest Power & Conservation Council's data needs. As each type of data is added to the online system, there must be some justification as to why it would be necessary for each of the participants to collect that data. These justifications can come from users, other Fish and Wildlife Program project data needs, or as directives from the Northwest Power & Conservation Council or the Bonneville Power Administration.

The Standard Query Method allows the user to pick all of the elements of the query from one screen (Figure 2). The query can be reached from the StreamNet home page (http://www.streamnet.org) by clicking on "Select your destination" and choosing "Data query." As an alternative the user can choose the Interactive Mapping applications which use GIS layers to map data.

Another feature of the fish data are independent data sets. These are set apart because they are submissions by non-participants and are not in the Data Exchange Format (DEF). They are also not considered priorities for StreamNet data collection, but the data may be important to researchers in the region.

FIGURE 2. StreamNet Query Screen

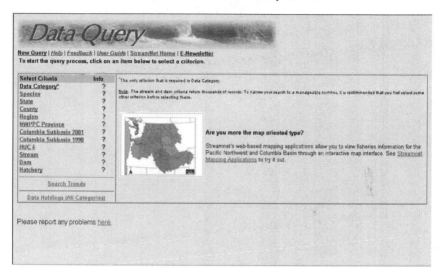

Maps and GIS

In addition to each piece of data being referenced, the data elements are also tied to geographic locations through a system called LLID (Latitude-Longitude Identifier) for rivers and streams. If the data has been generated from a large water body such as a lake or reservoir, they are assigned a Waterbody ID. These geo-references allow the data to be sorted geographically. As each data element is entered in the data exchange format, the LLID or Waterbody ID is assigned. These allow the user to generate maps on the fly. If the user doesn't have sufficient computing power, the StreamNet regional staff at the Pacific States Marine Fisheries Commission can generate these maps. Additionally, geo-referencing provides stream flow location and pinpoints waterbodies more accurately.

The Mapping feature allows users to build fish distribution maps via an interactive GIS layering system (Figure 3). There are also several pre-programmed maps available. The StreamNet GIS staff welcomes requests for specific maps that are not available through the query system or the catalog.

Public Education

The StreamNet Project website includes a Public Education section that features the Fish Coloring Book of children's fish art submissions. It also has a

FIGURE 3. Interactive Mapping Options

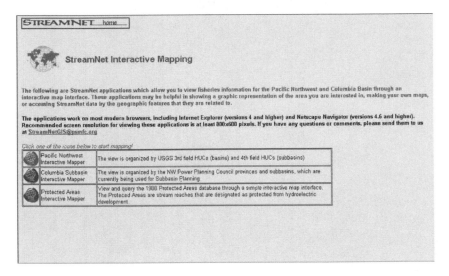

glossary, listing of fish species, fact sheets, interactive life cycles, ocean conditions and links for kids to follow to find more information. This section also contains links to curriculum on salmon and fish habitats.

FUTURE PROSPECTS

As the project grows and technology develops, StreamNet hopes to offer even more datasets, maps, and GIS layers through the online data and maps sections of the website. The project is striving to be the primary facilitator of information dissemination for the entire Columbia Basin Fish and Wildlife Program. Objectives for this goal are already being worked on with the independent data sets.

The Library will be increasing the number of documents that are available electronically. We have recently been named as the archive for the current subbasin planning initiative and will be creating digital archives of key references as well as the actual plans. Our recent expansion and remodel will allow us to increase our collection of documents and journals to support a wider range of topics related to the ecosystems of the Columbia River Basin.

REFERENCE

Steering Committee. 1996. StreamNet Project Summary. Unpublished submittal to the Bonneville Power Administration. Project no. 8810804, NPPC program 3.3A through 3.3E and 12.2.

Index

Access (direct), 32-33
Acid rain (national environmental data
   networks)
   Acidic Deposition Control Program
     and, 41
   Clean Air Act Amendments and, 41
   data sources of, 41-52
     LTER (Long Term Ecological
       Research) Network, 48-51
     MAB (Man and the Biosphere)
       Program, 43-48,54-57
     NADP (National Atmospheric
       Deposition Program), 42-43
     NAPAP (National Acid
       Precipitation Assessment
       Program), 40-42
     NTN (National Trends
       Network), 42-43
     overviews of, 41-42
   DOE (Department of Energy) and,
     41
   DOI (Department of the Interior)
     and, 41
   EPA (Environmental Protection
     Agency) and, 41
   future perspectives of, 52
   historical perspectives of, 38-41
   NAPAP (National Acid
     Precipitation Assessment
     Program) and, 40-41
   NASA (National Aeronautics and
     Space Administration) and,
     41
   NOAA (National Oceanic and
     Atmospheric Administration)
     and, 41
   overviews of, 37-38
   reference resources for, 51-57
   USDA (Department of Agriculture)
     and, 41

Acidic Deposition Control Program, 41
Acquisition processes, 10-12
ANSI/NISO Z39.50, 29-30
Archival processes, 10-12
Aronson, D., 73-87

Baldwin, V., 1-4
BioBot project, 63-67
BIODEG files, 75-76,78-79
BIOLOG files, 75-77
Bonneville Power Administration, 90-91

Cataloging (dynamic) approaches, 31-35
CEOS (Committee on Earth Observation
   Satellites), 25
CERCLA (Comprehensive Environmental
   Response, Compensation,
   and Liability Act), 86
CHEMFATE files, 75-78
Chemical information databases,
   73-87. *See also* Syracuse
   Research Corporation
   (chemical information
   databases)
Chemical Pointer Files, 73-75,85-86
Chen, R. S., 5-19
CIESIN (Center for International Earth
   Science Information Network),
   5-19
CIS (Coordinated Information System),
   90
Clean Air Act Amendments, 41
Collection scope issues, 23-25
Columbia River Basin (StreamNet
   Project), 89-94. *See also*
   StreamNet Project

   95

Printed and bound by CPI Group (UK) Ltd, Croydon, CR0 4YY

17/10/2024

01775687-0012